501 **PAINTBALL**

TIPS TRICKS AND TACTICS

501 PAINTBALL

TIPS TRICKS AND TACTICS

BY DAVE "LANDSHARK" NORMAN

FOREWORD BY JESSICA SPARKS

TATE PUBLISHING & *Enterprises*

Published by Tate Publishing & Enterprises, LLC
127 E. Trade Center Terrace | Mustang, Oklahoma 73064 USA
1.888.361.9473 | www.tatepublishing.com

Tate Publishing is committed to excellence in the publishing industry. The company reflects the philosophy established by the founders, based on Psalm 68:11,
"The Lord gave the word and great was the company of those who published it."

Book design copyright © 2007 by Tate Publishing, LLC. All rights reserved.
Cover design by Leah Leflore
Interior design by Kandi Evans

Published in the United States of America

ISBN:978-1-60462-722-0

1. Special Interest-Paintball-Technique-Autobiography

2. Strategy
08.15.01

I would like to invest the years of work that
went into researching this book, that they may
enrich and inspire generations of players to come.

Thank you to my friends and
family, to Total Greif and my editors, for encouraging
my passion, watching my games, and inspiring my writing.

This is for Anastasia, for bearing with me.
Josh and Jake, the best support team ever.
My parents for their capable assistance.
And Westminster professors David Collins and
Carolyn Perryfor inspiring my madness.

FOREWORD

By Jessica Sparks—Paintball Political Advocate, Editor, and
Champion Player

A dedicated writer, photographer, world adventurer, sometimes-
teammate and always friend, Dave Norman is a widely published
paintball journalist and a recognized authority on the sport.
Through this book he shares his unique perspective on the great
game of paintball, and how to play it better and more safely. Dave
commands respect for his drive to succeed, and indeed, the energy
he brings to every challenge.

I recall games when, disregarding thoughts of night critters we
might encounter, we belly-crawled through rocky backwoods. On
one such deeply shadowed night, I realized how seriously Dave
takes our sport. We flanked a heavily defended position as pyro
transformed surrounding forest, bunkers, and players into surre-
alistic images—a modern-day "Apocalypse Now". Dave, intensely
mission driven, led the squad forward with true dedication to tactics and safety.

As true, devoted paintball players, we are all rugged individu-
alists. We step onto the field of play as warriors of old, facing the
challenge to see who, indeed, will survive.

Whether we're swarming the Oklahoma hills on D-Day,
hammering the air-filled bunkers, or working on yet another issue
of *Action Pursuit Games*, I know Dave is giving the game all he has,
every minute, every second. He does that throughout this guide,
bringing a decade's experience to bear on playing better paintball.

I commend to you this excellent sport, and urge you to enjoy

Dave's book for the window it opens into the world's most thrilling, demanding, intricate game.

PREFACE

By Marc Gottfried—NPPL Referee, Referee Trainer, and
Paintball Writer

This weekend I'm attending a large event and I heard something that really made me smile. Paintball is now the second most participated in "extreme" sport in the world with over ten million participants in the US alone. Previously, we were in third place just under skateboarding and in-line roller-skating. I can remember a few years back when we overtook mountain biking and I thought to myself how incredibly far the sport has come in the years I've been fortunate enough to be involved.

It's a strange sport, even for the so-called extreme category. People jump off buildings with parachutes, surf and sail simultaneously, and even dive to great depths without the convenience of oxygen, but as I sit on the turf surrounded by all these little balls and look up at the grandstands I can't help but shake my head. It's strange, but also strangely addicting! My money, time, and imagination are consumed by this activity and I couldn't be happier.

It's like tag, Risk ®, chess, and dodge ball all rolled into one. The intricacies of paintball attract people from all walks of life, while the sport's fundamentals instantly level the playing field, making it challenging and open for absolutely anyone to join. The intriguing thing is that while the participants are from such varying backgrounds, they all seem to share much the same personality traits and values. Paintball is a team sport, and I mean that on so many different levels. It obviously builds leadership and the ability to work with others, but besides that, there is a "team" kind of quality to the interactions between players, refs, field owners, and spectators like I've never seen. A giveaway glimpse of a telltale piece of paintball clothing in an airport or restaurant is all it takes to start a friendly conversation between two players who have never met before.

A guy showed up at the field one day with a camera. He said he was with the *Suburban Journals,* a local neighborhood paper, and was working on something to do with paintball. We sat and shot the breeze for hours and boy was he hooked! That man was Dave Norman, the author of this book. I've known him for several years now and I think he's learned more about the sport than I ever will. He's a friend, teammate, fellow writer, and skilled player! I'm honored to be a part of this production, and I'm sure it will help the sport grow. That's something we're both committed to, even though at this point it seems like we're on a runaway train.

Paintball has needed a lot of help to grow through the years, as it was definitely not always the popular activity that it is today. Long ago in New Hampshire, a couple characters decided to shoot each other with forestry marking pistols and laid the groundwork for a team-based sport that became a multi-billion dollar industry. The original draw was the paramilitary aspect, and paintball's first name was "The Survival Game," mixing the thrill of pursuit with elements of war, wilderness survival, and of course, Capture the Flag. Games were organized, teams formed, and eventually tournaments were scheduled. The paint was real, actual paint and not a washable non-toxic fill like it is today. The players cleaned up with turpentine, and risked injury due to the lack of paintball-specific safety gear. Camouflage was the clothing of choice and shop goggles "protected" players' eyes.

Companies began to produce upgraded parts for the marking pistols to make them more suitable for play. True paintball goggles, markers, and accessories came on the market as the sport grew into a nationwide phenomenon. Finally, the Nelson Company, maker of the Nelspot 007 forestry marking pistol, developed water-based paintballs for use in the sport and things began to expand at a much greater rate.

At one point, paintball decided that to become accepted in the public eye it would have to lose the camouflage, lingo, and most of the military feel. JT USA was a company which manufactured equipment for paintball and the motocross industries, and they featured both lines of products in their advertisements. This led to paintball players wearing the bright colors and extreme patterns of JT's motocross line. Shortly thereafter, paintball all but left the woods for the clean, manicured speedball court. Suddenly, this adult cocktail of tag and war became acceptable to parents everywhere and the mass influx of new players began.

We used to dream of the day when paintball would be considered mainstream—whatever that really means. Our only options to buy equipment were mail order or a long drive, and we joked that you might be able to buy a case of paint at Wal-Mart some day. Now things have changed all around, and unfortunately the Internet and large chain stores have brought the demise of many independently owned paintball stores. In one way it warms my heart that droves of kids are being exposed to the sport, but I'm also sad that the "skate shop" era is gone.

Technology made electronic paintball markers possible and increased rates of fire to a blur. The modern colors, sounds, and excitement of paintball can be seen on the likes of ESPN, Fox Sports Net, and the Outdoor Life Network. Spectators have favorite pro teams that they root for in grandstands that hold thousands while an announcer calls the play-by-play. I never thought this day would come.

Where will we go from here? I fully expect paintball to become the number one extreme sport in the world within the next ten years. I hope you come try paintball in all of its many forms. Whether you enjoy purely recreational play (which is where my heart lies), crawl through the woods in a ghillie suit, contemplate strategy with your teammates, or rise to the top of the pro leagues and play on television, paintball has something to offer you. Above all, the camaraderie, entertainment, and pure adrenaline of this crazy sport will draw you in and keep you for life.

DISCLAIMERS & INDEMNIFICATIONS

The material contained in this book, including tips, tactics, recommendations, instructions, procedures, operations, and suggestions, has been collected, developed, researched and tested in the most thorough manners available at the time or incidentally encountered during the course of the book's research. It is presented here for informational value only, and the writers, editors, distributors, agents, and other persons involved with this book absolve responsibility for the use or misuse of contained or suggested material, any damages to person or property that result from the use or misuse of contained or suggested material, any criminal damages caused through the use or misuse of contained or suggested material, and any criminal punishments accrued directly or indirectly due to the use or misuse of contained or suggested material. Readers are reminded to consult owner's manuals for markers and accessories, use only ASTM-certified products and only within their intended methods of use within prescribed guidelines, and to consult certified airsmiths, referees, field owners, and other experts before implementing any measure, improvement, modification, or other practice or procedure. The best guide is often common sense, something the writers and others involved with this book cannot confer upon anyone or be held responsible for the lack thereof.

Before undergoing any change in diet, exercise, or lifestyle, consult a licensed physician. The author and other entities involved with the writing, research, production and distribution of

Contents

BASIC RULES OF PAINTBALL

1. Your goggles are to remain on at all times while on the field. Do not take them off for any reason. If your goggles fog up, call yourself eliminated and leave the field. Do not stick your fingers up into your goggles, take them off, or loosen them on the field! Only goggles specifically designed for paintball qualify as proper protection.

2. Keep your barrel bag on until the game starts, and put it back on immediately after being shot or when the game ends. There is no reason to have it off before the game starts. Putting it on again is a signal to the other team that you are eliminated, which will help prevent you from being shot after calling yourself eliminated.

3. Listen to the referee's instructions. They will explain the game format, special rules, special concerns, and start and end the game. If they tell you that you are eliminated, plug your marker and leave the field immediately. The ref's call is always final.

4. You are eliminated when hit anywhere on your body or marker, and the ball leaves a splat the size of a US quarter or larger. Bounces do not count as eliminations; neither does spray. This rule may vary slightly from field to field—be sure to check with the local referees.

5. When eliminated, immediately install your barrel cover, put your marker over your head, and leave the field. You may call "Hit!" or "Out!" but may not talk to your teammates, or your opponents. Failure to remove yourself from the game immediately will result in a penalty.

6. Only true semi-automatic markers and pump markers are allowed. Fire control modes such as "full auto" and "burst" are allowed on some fields and at some events, but are generally considered very dangerous and in violation of insurance regulations, and are thus banned in most places.

7. All markers must abide by the field velocity limit. Never more than 300 feet per second (fps), field speed limits may vary between 250fps and 300fps—the speed to which all paintball goggles are rated for adequate protection. Chronographs are provided for you to check and alter your velocity, and players are encouraged to check it periodically during the day.

8. All players must sign a waiver before taking the field. This may include spectators who want to don goggles and watch the games from the sidelines on fields without netting. Players under 18 will need a parent or guardian to co-sign, and should download and fill out the waivers at home and then bring them to the field.

9. Alcohol and drugs are not permitted under any circumstances. These substances are normally banned from the premises entirely, and players found under their influence may be ejected, for safety reasons, without refund.

10. Physical contact, fighting, and profanity are not allowed. Paintball is an all-age, family-friendly sport! Let's keep it strong, by fostering a safe and fun environment!

WOODSBALL

Woodsball is the domain of the sniper, where ambushes and stalking come into their own and camouflage serves a purpose. Paintball's roots are in woodsball, and it is still the most popular format across the country. The only facilities required for a woodsball field are privately owned woods, a road to the spot, and a place to control admission.

All games were held in the woods in the early days, and events like the "World Cup" precursor to the "NPPL World Cup" were held on forested fields up until the late 1990's. Woodsball is the genesis of scenarios and big games, and spawned the speedball format that took paintballers from the bosom of nature to chaotic inflatable fields. Much of the original allure was the element of stealth, and the ability for competitors to move undetected around a field before engaging friends from behind natural cover—to engage our competitive instincts in an atavistic way. It's only natural for many players to imagine they are soldiers trapped behind enemy lines and the like, the idea of which gave rise to the many military-themed scenario games we have today.

Since flag stations are seldom within direct sight of each other, players can sprint at the start signal undetected and unmolested by hailstorms of paint—right from the start you have the option to be as sneaky as you like. The pace of play is by no means slow, but with large courses and time limits between twenty minutes and an hour, there is ample time to set up ambushes and adventurous flanking maneuvers. Some strategies still involve leaving a contingent of players, traditionally newbies, behind to guard the flag station in the likely event that an opponent makes it past your team and all the way to your end of the field without getting tagged.

Stealth and cunning mix with foresight and no small measure of blind luck in woodsball games.

The general format of these games is capture the flag, where each team tries to cross to their opponents' base and capture their flag, then return it to their own base for the win. Exciting variations, many explained in the "Games We Play" chapter, include search and destroy missions, hunting style missions, rescue operations, and a host of other scenarios.

Any .68 caliber marker that shoots safely can be used in any paintball game, but the advantages of high cyclic rates that tournament markers demonstrate in speedball do not completely carry over to the forest. The ranges of engagement vary from point-blank to thirty yard long-ball shots between the trees; given the underbrush, you can get a lot closer to your opponents than you may think, even while they're shooting continuously at you. The markers normally used in the woods are black, and have shirked the arms-race-need for the electronic operating systems that revolutionized speedball. Stalwarts of the pneumatic age who distrust batteries and favor a marker that can take hard use find comfort in the rugged, mechanical, and nearly indestructible gear they carry through the shadows at woodsball fields.

Many players choose to wear camouflage, and when they bother to carry extra paint, often use harnesses that carry tubes horizontally rather than vertically. Remote setups let woodsball players carry their air in the center pouch of these harnesses, which helps them bring their markers to bear more quickly during ambushes! Boots rule the trails, and bug spray is mandatory in most areas.

Formal scenario games grew from popular themes in woodsball, and true to their roots, remain almost exclusively in the forest. Military themes such as D-Day re-enactments, Vietnam battles, the siege of "drug plantations" and other fantasy scenarios, come to life in pine forests, jungles, and desert fields around the world every weekend. Rugged terrain adds to scenario games' appeal, and players can go all out with ghillie suits and custom off-road vehicles—you'll never see a scale recreation of a Schutzenpanzerwagon rolling through an NPPL tournament, but you will in scenario games!

Many fields augment trees, gullies, and other natural cover with manmade bunkers. Clean, discarded plastic and steel barrels and large cable spools dot many woodsball fields. Like finding an ancient civilization nestled under an Amazonian jungle canopy, there are many woodsball fields with complete villages built from salvaged lumber and backwoods engineering. Big production fields construct castles and entire towns that feature paved streets and abandoned cars. The adventure lies in the game, but also in exploring these amazing facilities.

Woodsball players are skilled at sneaking up on their opponents, reading the topography of the land, and taking cover behind anything that will stop a paintball. The very first paintball game that involved more than just Hayes Noel and Charles Gaines hunting each other was an every-man-for-himself format where each of several players had flags at their personal starting point in the forest. The goal was to capture as many of their color flags from these positions as possible, and use cattle marking paint pistols to shoot their opponents. The winning player did not shoot a single paintball in the entire game, and won instead by strategy and stealth. This defines the woodsball experience: matching wits player vs. player in a rich environment set against oftentimes beautiful, largely natural, scenery.

Welcome to playing in the spirit of paintball's founding fathers. From here you can explore scenario games or strike off for the speedball field, and always find a walk-on group that will welcome you back to the forest.

Selecting a good side to start from is generally not important, as most referees will have you play a given field twice: once from each end. Even when you might only get one shot at the field, seldom is there enough of a one-side-advantage to warrant great worry over which end you take. Thus, when given the option, choose to start from the far end. Your teammates might whine about the walk, but they can handle it. Remind them of the tactical advantage in starting at the far end: you get to walk the length of the field, see all of the bunkers, note all of the features…Casual players seldom invest time and effort in walking and mapping fields for rec play, so walking the entire thing on your way to the start station provides a great opportunity to plan moves and get a feel for the layout. Your opponents won't have this advantage!

Be aggressive! Many players like the pace of woodsball games, citing that this format presents a great challenge to the mind, wits, and spirit. Woodsball offers countless opportunities for sneaking around, coordinating small group movements, running in sheer panic, and running in sheer joy. When many players are overly cautious of being ambushed or getting hit, those with the fast-and-loose mentality often take control of the field. So don't just camp out in one spot…give your mind the workout it deserves as you dominate with speed and cunning.

Stick bunkers, such as brush piles and stacks of logs and limbs, generally stop most (but not all!) paintballs. When you engage an opponent in a stick bunker, look for small holes in the bunker and straight paths between logs and twigs. Shoot those lanes, and you can usually get a ball on them.

You can create these holes by finding a section of the bunker that is filled in with only very thin twigs, dry sticks, and other easily broken material. Shoot a continuous stream of paint at this spot to break the twigs and clear a path for your paint to get at the opponent inside!

Analyze the field's topography. Bear in mind that dry creek beds make excellent routes around the field. If the walls are high enough, or you can crawl low enough, consider using them as a conveyance to sneak behind their lines. Remember as well that it is far easier to defend a hill from invaders than it is to try to win an uphill battle—plan strategies so that you capture and hold the high ground!

Some topography lends itself more to training than playing

Walk the field before the game, if possible—this probably means getting to the field before the rest of the group, or at least, getting ready before them. Wear your goggles, as there may be booby traps in place already, or left over from another day, and in case a game starts on an adjacent field—paint doesn't stop at the tapeline! Look for key bunkers, and any props or booby traps the event organizers put out. Get a feel for how the hills roll, the location of briar patches, and where creeks meander. When you find a great hiding place, perfect bunker, or nice observation point, make a note of it in reference to exceptionally tall trees or its position relative to creeks, structures, or other features of the land and field. This way you can find that place fast when you are under stress.

Use field conditions to predict the distance of engagement. Thickly wooded fields with dense undergrowth generally find players engaging each other at ten to twenty yards. Pine forest fields and other fields that have very little brush see engagements from farther away, with the density and type of bunkers largely determining the standoff range between opponents. You can adjust your tactics accordingly, as thick brush is better for hiding sneaky maneuvers and open fields are better for using carefully aimed long shots to control the field. Though your barrel length has nothing to do with range, you might consider the distances you will face before deciding whether or not to use any backspin-imparting barrels and devices.

Acquire a map of the field and study it carefully, or make one as you walk the field. Note the reinsertion zones, dead zones, and supply depots (such as air fill stations or paint vendor stations). Correlate these locations in a meaningful way when you walk the field before the game, and pay close attention to where you have to go when eliminated from various positions around the field. Also note all hazards, such as cliffs, barbed wire, boulder fields, cactus patches, and other places you want to avoid.

Hangernaid uses high quality relief maps to plan his epic battles at Oklahoma D-Day

Bunkers often have holes, cracks, nets, or other places that you can see through. Look for these observation points in woodsball play and speedball games alike. Be aware that a wild shot may come through the opening, but use it to keep an eye on the game while ducking incoming paint.

Certain rule sets have double standards when it comes to playing these holes. Some rules state that you cannot stick your barrel through a hole in a bunker, but may allow you to shoot out of the same hole so long as your muzzle doesn't poke through ("break the plane of the bunker," in some jargon). Others prohibit you from shooting out of the hole in any way, but rarely prohibit you from shooting into such a hole in an opponent's bunker!

Bunker walking, or "ghost walking," is very useful in speedball, and a great tactic for woodsball as well. Look for bunkers that align, usually in a diagonal manner, to obstruct your opponents' view of a certain "lane" on the field. While you may be shot from the sides, you can often advance down these lanes while protected from head-on opponents when you use these bunkers.

When engaging a single opponent head on in woodsball, shuffle sideways until you put a large tree, impenetrable bush, bunker, etc. between you and your opponent. Now, run straight towards the opponent, using the distant and intervening obstacle to shield you from paint and notice. Find a suitable bunker that provides an angle on your opponent, and run directly to it after you leave this blind alley.

Surrender rule. There is no rule that automatically makes you surrender to another player, but most fields have a rule that prohibits shooting players less than twenty feet away (for instance) during recreational games. When you close to less than twenty feet of an opponent, the surrender rule says you must give them the option of surrendering before you shoot them. This is a good courtesy to practice anywhere you play recreationally, whether there is a rule to enforce it or not—it's playing with honor, and the difference between respect and abuse. Only when the opponent tries to continue playing should you shoot him.

When should you shoot a player who might surrender? Watch for them to try shooting you, and as soon as they bring their marker to bear (which is different from raising it over their heads) or reach for the trigger, shoot them. Some players will freeze and not move, for lack of any better idea what to do. Experienced players will give them "to the count of three" to leave their base, put their marker over their heads, etc. Most of these players shoot on two, just to make sure their opponent isn't going to spin and try to go out in a blaze of glory.

Having a solid "command voice" will engender respect and obedience on the field, and help you assert yourself in the game. Good leaders have strong voices that inspire confidence among their team and fear in their opponents. Speak clearly, with a deep tone, at a slightly louder volume than everyone else. The command voice is a powerful leadership tool, so long as you never berate other players and only assert yourself as much as needed to organize strategies and execute maneuvers. Players are likely to follow suggestions and instructions from a person with an authoritative voice and a confident tone.

Eliminate players with your command voice when you invoke the surrender rule. Say loudly and confidently, without screaming or having your voice crack, "surrender now." You are in charge of this scenario, so act like it! Speak powerfully and do not give them an option, an "or" condition, or any other leverage; they must surrender, they must do it now, and there is no other choice.

Who is on your team? A simple rule of thumb is to look

towards your opponents, wherever they are at the moment. If you see the back of the player in front of you, then he is aiming in the direction of your opponents and is likely on your team! If you're shooting at the same adversary, odds are you're on the same team; it's better to wait and make sure than eliminate one of your teammates!

Mark yourselves in an obvious manner, if you don't mind trading a little stealth for a bit of security. Your gear bag should carry several colors of marking tape, the thin plastic tape used around construction sites. Find the roll of tape in your team's color, and tie it around both arms on each teammate. Also tie it around each of your hoppers. Now you can identify your teammates from either side, in front or behind, and in just about any physical position. When the action heats up and some of you flank, others crawl, and "that guy" runs screaming straight into their fort, you will be able to easily identify your teammates and avoid friendly fire!

Look for hopper covers, arm bands, or other identifying marks before you start shooting! Take an extra few seconds to positively ID your target before you start shooting…there will still be plenty of time to hit him. It is often hard to identify snipers and scouts, and you really don't want to hurt your team by taking out your own shadow warriors!

For positive identification from the rear, where most of the threat comes from when you play with newbies or folks who have not played with your team before, you can put a large cross of your team's colored tape on the back of your jacket. Your camouflage is still effective to your opponents, who mainly see your front or side, but the players who hide in the rear for most of the game will be able to tell that you are "friendly" when they finally charge to the front.

Many of these players open up on anyone they see in front of them, including their own players, out of fear or simply not knowing any better. Use the tape cross trick to avoid becoming your teammates' "easy out!"

Acquire an extra armband. Keep it in your pocket, or tied loosely around your weak-hand-wrist (if you are right handed, your left hand is your weak hand). When you come around blind corners, such as around the walls of a fort or when you clear buildings or other structures, hold the armband in your hand and stick it around corners before stepping around, while yelling "blue coming through," or whatever your color is that day. It takes a while for your hopper cover or armband to come into view, and by that time you are likely wearing an entire hopper's worth of paint.

Coordinate a solid color hat, bandana, or other head covering to your team's armband color. This is not necessarily a valid form of identifying yourself in place of armbands or hopper covers, but your teammates are likely to hesitate before shooting at you if they see you wearing their team color—the goal is to make them hesitate long enough to see your armband! The extra moment this buys could be all you need to prevent friendly fire. The better you identify yourself, the less likely you are to get shot by your own team.

The commander, in scenario games, or the player who takes a natural command in recball games, is one of the most important players on the field; protect him at all costs. Other important players in scenario games are "medics," "demolition experts," players carrying paint cannons or "rocket propelled grenade" units, props, etc. Unless you are one of these important people, they are more important than you. When sharing a bunker with such players, you should take more chances than them.

You should be their eyes and ears so they know what is going on without risking getting hit. Should the commander be eliminated, or the guy with the prop or the special weapon, your whole team gets hurt. Scout for these players, shoot cover fire for them, and help them however you can so that they are less likely to be tagged—you're helping the team, and that helps yourself!

When clearing buildings, caves, deep creek beds, or any other structure where your team loses sight with each other, have an identifying phrase that your front players call out at regular intervals so the rest of the unit knows where they are. The confusion of losing contact with your front players, or scouts, then seeing movement in bushes or in distant doorways, often leads to friendly-fire that eliminates your own personnel. Pick a phrase like "God bless America" or "Total Greif coming through!" and yell it so that your team knows how far ahead their scouts went. More complicated codes can carry specific meanings like "all clear," and "move up here now," without giving away the plan to any opponents in earshot.

Walk with your knees bent, and your weight on your back foot. As you step, use your leading foot to feel the ground for twigs that could snap, tripwires, mines, or ankle-twisting rocks and holes. By keeping most of your weight on your back foot, you can remove your lead foot and step elsewhere without losing your balance should you discover something you need to avoid. This prevents injury, giving away your position, and tripping booby traps!

Move your leading foot forwards to take a step, but before setting it down, move it in a half-circle outward. This will lay the grass and other brush aside so that you do not crush the stems as badly as tromping through the undergrowth flatfooted. Now it's hard for the other team to detect or track you (if you're sneaking around behind their lines), or tell how many of you moved through an area. It also quiets your step, so you avoid detection more effectively.

When you move through the area, the grass will rise back into place, largely obscuring your footsteps and making it harder for other players to track you. This also helps you to avoid rocks and other hazards.

Snow helps you track opponents wherever they go, so follow the footprints. More than just tracking the marks in the snow, however, read the prints to determine the size of their unit: look for only right, or left, prints, and count each different tread style you see, adding another person to the count if you see two different sizes of prints with the same tread style.

What do you know about their team? Do they have a lot of small, young players? Look for small footprints that do not sink as deeply into the snow as larger adult footprints, and if you find any, you know where the younger players went. Generally, the deeper the print, the heavier the person. Armed with this knowledge, recruit an appropriate seek-and-destroy squad to follow the tracks and engage the opponents.

When you need to run quietly, watch your path and avoid running through brush, stick piles, and bramble patches. Try not to land on twigs that snap or in piles of leaves that rustle. Watch the trail to avoid potholes, stumps, and other hazards. When you move quickly, put your foot down from heel to toe on the outside edge of the sole, then roll your foot inboard to flatten it against the earth. This is difficult at first, but is fast and incredibly quiet.

Fake them out. A small unit can make themselves seem absolutely huge in the woods when they spread over twice the area that they should normally control. When your opponents approach, take turns calling "blue team engage!" or "Robert, get 'em!" One of the other players should then shoot rapidly at your opponents, who will hear a command barked from one place and shots come from another. This makes them wonder how many players are out there, especially if they hear a "team," "unit," or "strike force" referenced in the command, as these words make the opponents think of groups of players instead of individuals.

Your teammates should shoot very rapidly and frequently call out to phantom players and phantom units, using phrases like "snipers, we have bad guys at …" Sure, you don't really have snipers out there, but the other guys think you do and will slow down accordingly—and when your scattered forces shoot from disparate positions while referring to phantom units, they'll wonder just how many guys are behind each of those bunkers and trees…

This tactic is also great for single players attempting to hold off a group. When your firepower alone can't stop them, scare them by calling out for phantom reinforcements. It probably won't work for very long, but should buy you some time for the real thing to show up.

Dry fire to conserve paint while keeping their heads down. Many beginning players cannot tell the difference in the sounds that markers make when they dry fire versus when they actually are shooting paint. Even experienced players naturally duck when they hear a marker discharging. But once they realize that no paintballs are splattering around them, they will get wise to your ruse and come out shooting. Now, shoot them with paint.

Tippmann shooters can slide the forearm of their Pro/Carbine markers forward to disconnect the hopper, or swing the hopper out of place on Model 98 markers, while players with power feeds can turn the feed plug upside down with a quick twist, blocking more paint from feeding into the chamber. Everyone can turn their marker upside down to prevent balls from actually feeding, and then pull the trigger quickly. Then when it's time, reconnect your paint supply and spray their squad!

Hold your frontline at all costs. Remember, your frontline is not static, and will not remain in place if all of its players retreat! There is great temptation in many woodsball players to fall back

Exotic markers with wild accessories make scenario gaming quite appealing

when the other force comes storming up the hill or a detachment of players flushes through a draw. Hold your line! They have to expose themselves while moving from bunker to bunker as they advance.

You, as a defender of the frontline, need only stay put in your bunker and shoot. Eventually you will be eliminated, but it is better tactically to be eliminated from the frontline than to retreat, pull the frontline back towards your end of the field, and then be eliminated close to your flag. Many positions can be held by sticking it out and not retreating.

For establishing a defendable frontline, pick a loose row of solid bunkers: large stick bunkers, "buildings," large spool-and-barrel arrangements, etc. Look for bunkers that offer protection from a large degree of the field, with special emphasis on side-protection from bunkers on each flank. When the opponents come, the only retreating any of your players should do is from tiny forward bunkers to these solid frontline bunkers. Hold tight, and whittle their team down!

Fill in the gaps in stick bunkers, cracks in plywood bunkers, etc, with snow. Snow can slow paint significantly, and sometimes break it. Reinforce your patch with twigs to help stop any paint they try to sneak through! During the rest of the year, you can fill holes in bunkers with brush or mud, but leaves generally do not work to stop paint.

Is that a solid bunker? Filling the gap is also a good way to psych them out, thinking that they cannot shoot through what appears to be a solid bunker…when they very easily could. Good patches turn bad bunkers into great ones, and help you stay in the game longer!

Some fields have a bewildering array of signs that mark dead zones, reinsertion points, safe areas, bathrooms, and even tank course traffic controls. Familiarize yourself with the signs around the field before the game so you know what area each marks, and how to respond to a given sign during a firefight (a blue triangle sign could mark a "helicopter drop point" for your team).

Your wrists are good places to wear a strap-on compass, a CO_2 12gram wristband, a watch, and a lot of other large objects that paintballs easily break on. If you wear anything of the sort, turn the dials or 12grams towards your body. This diminishes the accessible surface area a paintball can clip, and protects the face of your watch or compass.

Special Gear: Camo

Your camo is useless if you carry a shiny, bright-colored marker. The glint from the stainless steel and polished aluminum will make you stick out. This is fine if you play speedball, but has an adverse effect for players who rely on camo or ghillie suits for concealment. Removable matte-finish camo tape is a good way to cover your shiny marker when it comes woodsball time.

Tailor your camo to the season! The changing seasons bring changes in the color of the forest, from green in the summer to brown in the fall and white in the winter. There is camo for all conditions. Standard green BDU camo can actually make you stick out sometimes, such as during snowy winters or in light-colored desert, so have a variety of patterns in your closet.

Avoid wearing all one color, such as black. Camouflage works largely by breaking up the visual lines of your body so that your opponent's brain has a harder time recognizing your silhouette as the outline of a human. A solid color provides a clear outline of your body against multicolored backgrounds. Also, there are few truly solid color patches of forest, so you stick out in this way as well.

This is great concealment, and offers a good ambush position

Mixing similar pattern camouflage can help you blend in better, but mixing drastically different camo can seriously hinder your attempts to avoid detection. Matching camo turns your body into a blob, but a blob of homogenous and somewhat balanced disorder. The human eye is keen on picking up shapes by analyzing outlines and any straight lines contained in the object, as well as differences in shading. In this way, your camo can actually make your body stand out a bit from the background, as no background is as orderly as the swirls and splotches of color on your camo. Try wearing hunter's camouflage for pants and woodland military camo for your jacket, or a similar theme, to minimize how much of your body is the same color scheme and seemingly the same texture.

Beware of mixing drastically different camo styles, like woodland and digital tan, or black and white urban with anything else. This creates a hard line between where one type of camo ends, and the other begins. Eyes are attracted to hard lines, and this can make you stand out dramatically.

Augment your camo as you go. Few players have the patience to make, or money to buy, a quality ghillie suit. But, you can reap the benefit of some ghillie principles by tucking small leafy branches under your belt and wrapping leafy vines comfortably around your legs and arms. This adds a three dimensional appearance to your otherwise smooth outfit, and helps in breaking up the lines of your body. You may not look like a bush, or anything in particular at all, but the goal is to simply break up your silhouette. …not necessarily masquerade as shrubbery.

The best place to hide is under a dense bush that grows limbs or wide leaves approximately eighteen inches above the ground. Crawl into the shadows under these bushes or vines that grow between logs and the ground, and the three dimensional aspect of having the bush in front of or over you will help hide your form. You also benefit from the shadows it casts on your clothing, and from the psychological benefit that many players look for opponents behind concealment…not in it.

Pay attention to shadows. Our eyes detect light reflected off of objects, and shady areas are darker because less light reaches our eyes from there than from the surrounding areas. Thus, our pupils are adjusted for the brighter light conditions, and we do not see shadowed objects very clearly. Use this to your advantage when hiding from opponents by crawling through shadowy areas and setting up ambushes from shade that borders well-lighted areas (such as open fields).

GHILLIE SUITS

Ghillie suits give players extreme concealment

Ghillie suits are quite handy for paintball snipers, special operations units, and players who are sent to infiltrate opposing camps during scenario games. They are not practical for open play, though rec ball woods games offer a good opportunity to test your ghillie before the next scenario game.

Ghillie suits originated in Scotland, where master hunters and guards used early ghillie suits to hide in the orchards and forests of noblemen. These guards thwarted poachers and trespassers. Nowadays ghillie suits are used by Marine Recon snipers, Navy SEAL's, SWAT team snipers, and other military and law enforcement professionals who rely on the ultimate in concealment to carry out their missions. Industrious paintball players wear them to get the drop on opponents in the forest, where the limited range of paintballs and dense undergrowth combine to make ambush distances frighteningly close.

This is how you build a ghillie suit. Gather essential materials: an old camouflage jacket and pants, or to make a ghillie hide, a bolt of burlap one foot wider than your arm span and two feet longer than your height. This will serve as your outfit or hide. Ghillie suits built from camouflage clothing are often easier to move in and are effective from multiple body positions (such as kneeling or sitting) where your chest might be exposed. The hide offers the ultimate in prone concealment for crawling, prone position ambush, and ease in setting up a blind to hide behind or for concealing a cave entrance or hole.

Gather enough burlap to produce one hundred fifty to two hundred burlap strips that each measure two inches wide by eight to ten inches long. Vary individual width slightly, and the length by several inches, between pieces. A person 5'8" tall with a 34" waist will need at least one hundred seventy five burlap strips. Have enough material on hand to make a few dozen strips more than you estimate needing.

Burlap can be purchased from large lawn care stores, as many landscapers use large sheets of it to cover grass seed. Poke around farm supply stores and grain mills to find discarded burlap bags you can cut up. If you can purchase camouflage-painted burlap that hunters use to make blinds, that is a good start. Otherwise, the plain brown burlap will work fine.

After securing your burlap, scout the area where you will use your ghillie most. Pay attention to the colors found there, and think about the effects of changing seasons. Wooded fields in the Midwest, east, and much of the south maintain a healthy level of brown on the forest floor year-round, with seasonal undergrowth in varying shades of green. Pine forests generally have less green undergrowth, and stay brown year-round, while desert areas generally stay tan or light brown with shades of red for most of the year. Take notes on the colors you find, and then go to your local hardware store for spray paint.

Purchase at least three different colors, or shades, of paint. Your burlap is brown to begin with (the camouflage burlap will benefit from light touchup work just to break up the similar hues of the dyes they use), so you will need to add whatever other colors you find at your field. Many places carry paint specifically designed to make camouflage patterns: get this if you can. Choose paint that says "matte," or "dull," and go for subdued earth tone colors. Stick with cheap paint: anti-rust specialty paint will not do you any better, will cost more money, and takes longer to dry.

Before you leave, buy at least two bottles of "fire retardant spray," and ask for it specifically. This is a chemical spray that takes highly flammable material (like burlap, spray paint, and spray painted burlap) and makes it significantly less flammable. This is very important, as many woodsball games involve smoke grenades, smokers, and other seemingly benign sources of open flame and concentrated heat.

Acquire a needle and at least one full spool of black thread, fifteen feet of rope, and earth-tone yarn. These are the last of your needed materials.

Tie the rope between two trees or posts so that it hangs over grass or dirt (you do not want the paint dripping onto concrete). Hang the burlap, shake the spray paint, and using one bottle in each hand, paint the burlap with random stripes and dots. Do not paint too heavily on one area, and remember: when you cut this up, any patterns you paint will be lost in the cutting. Use all the colors at your disposal, then let it dry for ten minutes. Flip it over and repeat. Leave a bit of the brown burlap showing.

If you use camo burlap to begin with, spray considerably less paint but still add your own highlights and spots. For ghillie suits based on the hide concept, spray the hide in as random of a camo pattern as you can manage with the paint you have available.

Now spray all of the burlap, both sides, and your base material (jacket and pants or shroud) with the fire retardant spray.

When everything is dry, cut the burlap into strips two inches wide by eight to ten inches long. Arrange the camo jacket and pants, or shroud, on the ground as if you are wearing them. You will need to sew the strips "up," by placing a strip on the jacket and sewing on the bottom end. This way gravity will pull the other end down and away, giving the material a three-dimensional aspect that creates natural texture and shadows. Sew the strips in jagged lines on every outside surface of the jacket and pants or shroud, putting them approximately five inches above and two inches to the side of each other. The shorter strips can be used around the collar, cuffs, armpit, and crotch areas to prevent the material from bunching up uncomfortably or getting in the way of your hands and goggles.

When you are finished, take the remaining material and consider making a head shroud (a flap that sews to the collar, or top of the hide, and flops forwards over your head when you are in the prone position) or marker ghillie.

To add ghillie to your marker without altering it in any way, make a marker shroud out of burlap (like the hide or the head shroud) to put over your marker, or dedicate one hopper to having burlap super glued to it.

Make your ghillie even more effective by scrunching up the dangling fabric, creasing it, and fraying the edges. This gives it even more of a three-dimensional appearance, rather than being just a collection of flat strips. It also creates natural shadows and imparts the sense of depth and texture found on the forest floor. The colors are intended to blend into the background, so when players look for "color" they are fooled, and when their brains search their perceptive fields for recognizable shapes (hopper, leg, arm), their brains read only meaningless texture (think "static" like on a scrambled television channel).

In 2003 the author conducted an experiment at Westminster College on the effects of camouflage and the process by which the human brain identifies objects and is fooled by simple tricks. The conclusion of the experiment, and associated meta-analysis, supported these explanations of how camouflage and ghillie suits trick the brain.

Only one trick remains for the eye to detect a player in ghillie: movement. Stay perfectly still when opponents are looking for you, and rely on the craftsmanship of your outfit to take care of the rest.

Leave bait in an open area, such as the middle of a trail or a small clearing. Few people can walk past a dollar bill without stopping to pick it up, or a pod without at least pausing to look at it. When their eyes are down, so is their guard: shoot them before they can look up and spot you. Small, shiny or brightly colored objects are great for trails you know are heavily traveled. For larger areas, such as clearings (but not near bunkers or doors they can duck into!), try something bigger. Remember that size and color matter to attract attention, and if you use a dollar bill, put a rock on it so it doesn't blow away.

Highly respected paintball sniper Knight Owl likes to paint plastic Easter eggs gold and leave them on paths. Scenario players are particularly attuned to things that could be props worth points, and will go out of their way to pick up such bait. When they bend over, Knight Owl shoots them. Beware that whatever you leave might get stolen by the player you ambush, but if not: pick it up after you leave the area.

William Shatner relies on bodyguards in ghillie...notice one in the background, standing up?

Cannons

Paintball cannons are inherently dangerous. They propel large, or numerous, objects, frequently at high speeds that are hard to regulate. The materials available to the average hobbyist are generally rated for water pressure, not gas pressure, which has different properties—compressed gases are much more dangerous than water under pressure. The tips below are for research purposes only, and anyone attempting to build a compressed air powered cannon should use only parts rated for the gas pressures involved. Use extreme caution, common sense, and proper safety procedures any time you work with or around compressed gas.

The basic theory behind paintball cannons is to use a rapidly expanding gas to propel an object (a paintgrenade, a cluster of paintballs, a smoke grenade...) towards a non-human target. Just like your marker uses expanding CO_2 or compressed air to propel a paintball out of a barrel, paintball cannons harness the expansion of gas to propel their payloads out of barrels. The essential components of cannons are the air source (12 gram disposable powerlets, constant air CO_2 tanks, or compressed air bottles), the air reservoir where pressurized gas is held in readiness for shooting, the firing valve, the barrel, and a pop-off valve to guard against over-pressurization.

To understand how a cannon works, trace the gas from the tank to the atmosphere. When you pressurize the cannon, air escapes from the power source into a holding area. When you open the firing valve, the air escapes to an area of lower pressure (as all compressed gasses do), which happens to be the chamber of your cannon.

Here it encounters a roadblock: the projectile. So long as the force required to move the projectile is less than the force required to blow a hole out of the side of your barrel (this is why you should only build with pressure rated materials!), the gas will seek to lower the pressure in the chamber by increasing the chamber's volume through pushing the projectile forward.

When you introduce the pressurized gas to the chamber quickly by "dumping" it (flipping the valve quickly), the gas will quickly push the projectile out of the barrel. The faster the valve opens, and the higher the gas pressure, the higher the velocity of the projectile…exactly how your marker works!

A critical component of this process is the seal that the projectile makes around the bore of the cannon. As gas always seeks the path of least resistance to areas of lower pressure, you must make sure that the gas can only escape the cannon by pushing the projectile. If your payload is loose objects, such as paintballs, you will need to make a gas check that provides a solid barrier between loose paintballs and the expanding gas, and that seals well around the bore so that gas cannot escape around the edge of the gas check. Odd shaped projectiles, or cylindrical projectiles that are too small to seal the barrel by themselves, need the help of a gas check as well.

Familiarize yourself with the field's rules pertaining to cannons and special gear before you go to the scenario game, or try that field for open play. Some fields ban all projectile devices (such as slingshots, cannons, and mortars) other than recognized paintball markers, while others have such rules as the indirect fire rule and 45-degree angle of inclination rule.

These rules state, essentially, that cannons are not to be used against players (only tanks), and mortars intended for antipersonnel use must be inclined at least 45 degrees so the paintballs have a downward arc when they impact players.

Know the field's velocity and operating pressure limits well in advance so that you may be able to modify your cannon or mortar before the rush on game day!

Have your cannon inspected by a referee, and remember the referee's name. Quality referees will be able to advise you on the field-legality of your cannon. If another referee, or player, later questions you having or using the cannon, find the referee who inspected your cannon and bring the matter to him. By dealing honestly with the same person, simple miscommunications can be avoided. Always defer to the Ultimate Ref, or the highest ref appointed by the event coordinator.

Cannons shoot multiple paintballs simultaneously, or solid projectiles. Solid projectiles like paintgrenades are indirect engagement devices, meant to hit the ground or a tree and then spray paint onto players. Hitting a person with a solid projectile can have potentially deadly results.

Players can also sustain serious injury, or at the least, suffer serious pain, from taking a full load of paintballs from a cannon blast. To this end, never point paintball cannons directly at individuals, or engage any target that is closer than twenty yards away. Another benefit of following this safety rule: beyond twenty yards, your mortar's cluster of paintballs will spread out wide enough to take out the better part of an entire squad!

Paintball cannons should not use combustible gases, such as propane or aerosol, to propel their payloads. If the propulsion force comes from an exploding gas, the device is technically a firearm and legally regulated as such...and too dangerous for use in paintball. Cannons in our sport use only inert, non-explosive compressed gases released in a controlled manner, for propulsion—thus making their construction legal and increasing their safety.

Building a paintball cannon? Pay careful attention to the pressure ratings of all the materials you use. Steel pipe rated for high-pressure gas is ideal, and your couplings, fittings, and valves should be rated well above your intended operating pressures... and rated for gas pressure, not water pressure. Most commonly encountered iron pipe and PVC pipe will explode if subjected to the pressure of gas coming out of CO_2 bottles and compressed air systems. Know your material!

When you join components, such as threaded pipes and valves, use Teflon tape or liquid adhesives specifically designed for joining plastics (or metal, depending upon construction) in high-pressure gas devices. When using the liquid compounds, apply the solution to the first two rows of threads that will be engaged when you join the parts. This way the excess is spread throughout the threads from the first row to the last, and fewer air spaces in the threads exist, minimizing leaks.

Install pop-off and bleed valves in your cannon. These

can be purchased at most car parts supply stores and welding supply stores. They screw into your gas lines or directly into an air reservoir on your cannon. These valves open to jettison the gas if the internal pressure is too great, thus preventing deadly explosions. This is essentially what burst disks do in CO_2 tanks. Bleed valves allow you to lower the pressure in your cannon by venting excess gas before you encounter danger.

Trying to get multiple shots from a single 12gram CO_2 powerlet? This can be accomplished by installing a second valve in your cannon. All cannons have a "firing valve," that actually shoots the cannon. To get multiple shots from a 12gram, or to prevent excessive loss of air with a constant air bottle, install a second valve between the gas input and the reservoir. This cuts off the flow of gas into the air reservoir, while the firing valve cuts off the flow of gas into the chamber. You now can isolate the power source and get better gas efficiency!

Get more oomph out of your cannon by enlarging the passageway from air reservoir to chamber. Commonly encountered ½ inch ball valves are not as effective at suddenly, and evenly, venting the contents of an air reservoir as a ¾ inch or 1 inch ball valve.

Put the firing valve inline with the chamber, and as close to the chamber face as possible. Orient the reservoir behind the firing valve, inline with the barrel, if possible. Now your gas can flood immediately, and directly, into the chamber instead of swirling at bends and creating turbulence that slows down the rapid expansion you need for a powerful shot!

Many projectiles, such as paintballs and water balloons modified into paintgrenades, need a sabot to keep them from sticking to the bore and breaking in the barrel. A sabot is essentially a sleeve in which the projectile rests, with a gas check at the base to ensure proper operating pressures and optimal velocity. This sleeve keeps the payload from directly contacting the bore, which often causes the disintegration of the payload within the barrel.

Since gas checks add friction to the projectiles, and this friction often keeps them from sliding into the chamber quickly, many shooters use a ramrod to push the projectile back to the chamber.

Gas checks can be made very effectively from the Styrofoam material used in flower shops to stick artificial flowers in planters. This light, foamy material is easily shaped into a gas check, and upon exiting the barrel, has such a mass/volume ratio that it does not become a dangerous projectile. Often these gas checks are reusable if collected before they get stepped on!

Cut perfect gas checks quickly with a cutting die. Take the scrap barrel material, and cut three inches from its length. Use a metal or wood file to sharpen one end of this segment, filing down the outside edges so the inside diameter at the lip of the segment remains unchanged. Shape this die until the edge is uniformly sharp, and then use it to cut perfectly shaped and sized gas checks out of Styrofoam blocks and other blank material.

Solid projectiles, such as smoke grenades, seldom come sized perfectly to fit down your cannon's barrel. Purchase smoke grenades that are slightly undersized, and then construct a modified gas check with electrical tape. Face the fuse or pull pin end of the smoke grenade so that when inserted into the muzzle that end is the last part to slip inside. Wrap the electrical tape in a single-tape-width band around the opposite end of the projectile. Wrap enough tape that you form a seal around the bore that allows the projectile to slowly slide to the chamber by gravity alone.

By placing this modified gas check at the rear of the projectile, you get a seal around the propellant that is maintained for the longest possible time during acceleration. This improves gas efficiency.

Sabots are commonly made out of the cardboard tube found inside of toilet paper and paper towel rolls. When used in conjunction with the Styrofoam gas checks, they can form great sabots!

Size the sabot body to your bore by slitting it the length of the tube, then inserting the tube into your bore. Constrict or expand the tube until it makes full contact with the bore, and then tape it in place. Now you have a perfectly sized sabot!

Carefully cut the walls of your sabot almost the entire length from the mouth to the gas check. When the sabot leaves the barrel, air whipping around the projectile will attempt to separate the sabot from the payload. This is a good thing, as payloads should not contain any more matter than necessary, and clusters of paintballs need to disperse in the air so that targets do not suffer damage from sustaining multiple hits.

When you slice the walls of the sabot from the mouth down, you create petals that will open when the payload leaves the muzzle. The increased drag of the sabot will strip it away from your aerodynamic projectiles, and you can collect the sabot for possible reuse.

Loose paintballs will roll out of a sabot unless held in place, but they cannot be held in place in such a way that they remain tightly clustered in flight. Solve this dilemma with a piece of tissue paper. Fill your sabot with loose paintballs, and then put a piece of tissue paper over the open end. Tuck the tissue paper between the paintballs and the sabot, so that when the sabot slips into the barrel, the pressure will hold the tissue paper in place. Now the paintballs will not roll out of the sabot before you shoot!

Effective gas checks for sabots can be made from two layers of duct tape. After sizing the sabot body to the bore, put a square of duct tape around the "base" of the sabot. Put a second layer of duct tape over the first, then put a single square of toilet paper into the base of the sabot on the inside. This keeps the sticky side of the duct tape from clinging to the rearmost paintballs, or affixing the sabot to the paint/smoke grenade!

Ball detents for cannons? You can install a detent in a cannon with the right tools. Weigh the benefits and shortcomings of such modifications before committing to the task. When running with your cannon, there will be a natural tendency for the projectile to fall out of the muzzle…that's just the way gravity works. Loose paintballs need to be packed into sabots in such a way that they will not roll out of the barrel before you are ready to shoot, but sometimes loose sabots and loose smoke grenades will simply slide out without your knowledge. You can install a detent that puts pressure on the sabot or smoke grenade so that it will be less inclined to fall out.

Drill a 1/16 inch hole in your barrel, on a side where your hand and face will never be near, about 2.5 inches up from the base of the barrel. You should measure the position of the hole so that you have no more than one inch of space between the hole and the actual chamber face, so figure the position of the hole by measuring the distance between muzzle and the chamber face instead of measuring the outside of the barrel.

Acquire a small cotter pin, and pull the legs apart to a thirty degree angle. Slip the longer of the two legs into the hole, keeping the other leg on the outside of the chamber. Fill the hole with a type of plastic-safe epoxy glue, and then tape the exposed leg to the barrel by wrapping black electrical tape around it several times. Now take a smoke grenade and insert it into your barrel (remember to keep the shoulder of the modified gas check towards the muzzle), using a tamping rod to tamp it all the way back to the chamber face. This will form the detent in the optimal position to rub against your projectile, without poking it or getting in the way. The added side pressure should keep your projectile from sliding out of the barrel without adding any dangerous pressure spikes to the operating pressures.

Make ramrods out of a wooden dowel rod that is long enough to project out of your muzzle at least one inch when the pushing end is against the chamber face. This will give you the proper length to seat projectiles and still have enough ramrod to grip during use.

Narrow ramrod heads can pop paintgrenades or smash paintballs, so make the surface area bigger by screwing or gluing a small wooden disk or wooden hobby wheel (such as for wooden toy cars) to the ramrod. Be sure to pre-drill for any screws that you use, or else the rod may split.

Make paintgrenades out of the tubular balloons clowns use for balloon animals. Go to a party supply store and purchase these balloons, a tube of washable nontoxic finger paint, and a binder clamp. At home, mix the finger paint with water in a disposable bowl, using roughly two parts water to one part finger paint. Cut the balloons in half, and tie one end off in the sections that have two open ends. These will form the bodies of your paintgrenades, and will fit perfectly into a sabot for a 1.5 inch bore.

Fill the balloon segments with the paint by injecting the paint into them with a small hand pump from a paintgrenade making kit, a water balloon filling kit, or a turkey baster. Use the clamp to pinch off the ends while you reload the pump, and then tie the end off when you are done!

Nerf Vortex® missiles, shaped like miniature footballs with fins on a stick, are a popular projectile for paintball cannon crews. These are intended for use only against tanks or the sides of forts to "blow the fort" in a "rocket attack." Their size is optimal, and they fly far with good accuracy.

Nerf Vortex® footballs make great cannon ammunition—use them only against tanks and bunkers where there is no chance of hitting a player!

Mark your hit with a Nerf Vortex® round by filling a spare 100 round tube halfway with cheap shampoo or petroleum jelly. Add carpenter's chalk until the tube is ¾ of the way full, then thoroughly mix it to ensure that the chalk is evenly distributed throughout. Dip the nose of your Vortex® round in this solution, and on impact, it will leave a colored streak on the vehicle to prove you eliminated it.

SMOKE GRENADES

Smoke grenades are handy tools for scenario players, if used correctly. To make a smokescreen, which is only effective on days without much wind, you can plop a smoke grenade in front of your bunker and then escape while your opponents can't see you as clearly. To block most of their forward field of vision, throw one in front of their bunker.

They can be used to mark important bunkers, special props or other objectives, and to coordinate attacks on large fields. If you find a "hidden base," or just happen to find an isolated cell of opponents, mark their location with a smoke grenade. Tell your team before the game that if they see (give the color smoke you are carrying), they need to run to it and eliminate anyone they find there.

Tell your team that a certain color of smoke indicates your detachment is running out of players and needs reinforcements. Not only will the smoke signal to the rest of your team that you need help, but it will mark exactly where you are so they can get there fast!

Closely monitor field conditions, and only use smoke grenades when the fields are still wet with dew, rain, snow, or are otherwise at a low risk for fire. Check with the field owner to be sure that the field allows smoke grenades, and that the fields are "fire safe." Even then, do not throw a smoke grenade into a pile of brush, pile of leaves, or at anything that is flammable. Hard, open ground and short, green grass are ideal places to throw smoke grenades.

Use smoke grenades to "blow" bases. Arrange rules with the game coordinator and referees where a smoke grenade marks the "impact of an artillery round," or some such creative concept. Any player within a certain area of the smoke grenade is thus eliminated, and any player inside of a base that has a smoke grenade thrown against it is also eliminated. Do not throw smoke grenades into bases, foxholes, or blindly into areas where you think players might be gathered! This can set bunkers on fire, or catch players on fire, and lead to serious injuries…just throw the smoke grenade against a base's wall instead.

Extra smoke grenades can often be carried inside of paint tubes, and thus transported in your pack. By isolating the smoke grenades like this, you protect their pull pins and fuses from snagging or accidentally catching fire, either of which could cause them to combust while on your body. Carry them in the tubes for safety, and to help carry a lot of them with ease!

PAINTGRENADES

Paintgrenades are interesting offensive tools, and are great for clearing a room when you don't want to charge blindly into it. Pull the pin, or otherwise arm the grenade, and give it a hard toss into the room you need to clear. Throw it through an open window or door, and throw it at waist-level. It will likely go off when it hits a wall, and throwing it waist-high improves your odds of getting spray onto your opponents. Do not throw it at head-height, as it can impact goggles and knock them off.

A paintgrenade can eliminate a tank in some games. In these cases, throw the grenade at the intersection of the windshield and the hood. This joint will somewhat trap the grenade, and offers surfaces at two different angles for the fill to splash upon, whereas throwing it at the sides or rear only gives one surface to catch spray…and the grenade will likely bounce off and squirt on the ground instead of on your target. Also, if you get paint on the windshield, the driver is more likely to realize the tank is hit and stop immediately. Stand to the front of the tank, but off to the side and out of its path.

Turn paintgrenades into mines by tying tripwires around the rubber bands that keep them from going off until impact, and then tying the other end of the tripwire to a door or across a doorway or trail. Secure the paintgrenade to a stick or window with twine so that it will stay in place as the tripwire rips off its cap.

Hang other paintgrenades a few feet off of the ground with a tripwire running up to a hook, nail, or branch, then down along the ground. Pull the pin or remove the plastic wrapping. When the tripwire is stepped on, the grenade will fall. The impact knocks the rubber band off, or dislodges the BB inside the hose, and it sprays your unsuspecting opponent!

This squad is using a catapult to fling paintgrenades into a swarm of 2,000 players!

Paintmines can take out an entire squad if rigged correctly! Try installing them in a large bunker, such as the kind your opponents will likely put several players into. Put the mine in the middle, towards the front, so that players leaning out on the sides will not likely trip it. These sorts of command bunkers usually have players shooting out of the sides, but the mine should be tripped by a player in the center of the bunker...meaning that there will likely be at least two, maybe three, or even four players in the bunker when it goes off and gets them all!

Other popular places to put booby traps like this include doorways, windows or other prime shooting portals that you know players will use…and right under your team's flag! You can rig tripwires to set off paintgrenades when the flag is pulled, when a "discarded marker" is picked up, or in any number of other ingenious situations. Remember to only string tripwires at knee level and below, otherwise they pose the hazard of dislodging goggles.

See the Tech chapter for more on how to rig paintgrenades to function as mines and booby traps!

STRATEGIES

Establishing an ambush? Trying to plan what areas of the field will be used by special operations teams? While the action rages on one side of the scenario field, scouts and snipers should recon roads, paths, and assess abandoned bases for their future tactical use. Look for massive amounts of fresh footprints in the dirt to tell how the opposing team was positioned or where they moved. The fewer the footprints or the less a trail has been used, the less you should be interested in controlling it.

Look at bunkers and trees to tell if a base or other area has seen significant action. The amount of paint expended in the area will give you a feel for the amount of action that was seen there. Piles of paint from where players clumsily dumped pods while reloading indicate that any action was prolonged and intense—players don't often make that mistake when they're relaxed.

Determine where the paint came from: a part of the base that was heavily stacked with defenders will have a significant amount of paint on the walls, because attackers don't light up empty rooms. Now you know which parts of the base see the most action, where attackers come from, and can figure out how to allocate players to defend that position. Use this information to establish a strong defense or launch an effective attack if this area comes into play again.

Consult your list of upcoming missions, identify the base or area you just scouted, and see if there are any more operations that involve the area or areas close by. If so, consider laying an ambush for opponents who rush to the spot to assume control of the fort or terrain. Consider establishing ambush points on any major roads or trails, and report immediately back to your commander.

Choosing a good ambush point is a fine science. Look for valleys formed from steep hills that slope to a narrow path with little cover. This is an ideal ambush point, but is hard to find. For your average ambush, identify a heavily traveled road or trail and walk along it until you find either a solid bunker or thick undergrowth.

The bunker should shield you from view and incoming paint, and offer a peak at the path through a window or crack so that you do not have to hang your head out to scan for targets. Opponents will quickly realize where you are if you pop out of the bunker and blaze away.

Be prepared to hold your ground without snapping back into your bunker. Remaining opponents will sweep wide and flank you once you disappear behind cover, so you have to sustain your attack until you hit them all or your backup eliminates any remaining players.

Dense undergrowth offers a stealthy ambush point ideal for engaging single targets or groups of no more than four. An experienced scout can eliminate four players without detection, but this is very difficult. Undergrowth generally offers great concealment, but poor cover, as an intimidating amount of the paintballs shot your way will likely come right through the leaves and limbs to get you. Your main protection comes from concealment, the element of surprise, and then eliminating them all before they can get you.

Lay parallel to the path you are ambushing, not perpendicular to it. Line your body up with the path no less than two feet from the path and no more than eight feet away. Make sure you have a clear "window" to shoot out of, so that there are few or no branches between your muzzle and your targets—even though you want thick brush concealing the rest of your body. This window should be large enough to permit a wide angle of fire to sweep both sides of the trail, but not so large as to excessively expose your upper body to sight or return fire.

Perfect ambush spots have three elements. They are established along well-traveled paths, roads, or dry streambeds. They offer the ambushing players concealment with strong cover by effectively hiding them as well as stopping incoming paint. They offer little cover or concealment for the ambushed players to jump behind, should any make it through the initial contact. Look for locations that also offer you protected egress from the area, such as a streambed to crawl or run through after initiating first contact with a group you do not completely eliminate.

In the perfect ambush, you orient your body to point away from the direction of your targets' approach. The early warning of their approach is the sound of footsteps and voices. Your view should ultimately be of the targets' backs. They should approach you from the rear, so that your shot is on their backs as they pass by.

Do not move your head around looking for them; listen

for them to approach, and then wait patiently for them to cross your line of fire. As dishonorable as the idea may seem, your goal is to shoot each of the players in the back before they have any idea what is going on.

Wait until the last player in their party is in front of you with his back turned toward your muzzle before engaging. If the group is compact, work from one side to the other to eliminate everyone. If the players are staggered, shoot a well aimed shot at the farthest player and then engage the ones closer to you. This prevents a distant opponent from diving behind cover and coming to flank you.

Shoot for the middle of their backs, not their packs. Even honest players will often play on with a hit on their pack, simply because they do not feel it. In the heat of the action, the players will shoot you repeatedly before stopping to consider if they might have taken a pack hit. Everyone feels direct hits to the body, especially when their guard is down and they don't have adrenaline to numb the unexpected impact.

It will take a second for players to respond to being hit and understand the commotion of their friends yelping with surprise. They will instinctively whip around and look behind them to figure out where they were shot from, and the players you do not hit immediately will be looking for any piece of you to shoot at. You should put one paintball on each player in the time it takes them to respond, a second paintball on any player who continues to play, and then immediately stop shooting in case they have not yet figured out where you are.

Lay still, so that they cannot tell where you are. Dishonorable players will respond to being ambushed from the rear by shooting you anyway, or at least telling their teammates where you are on their way to the reinsertion point. You do not want them to know where you are, as even an honorable player will reinsert and come straight back to get you!

When your partner gets hit, as often happens with sniper teams or two man patrols, do not move. Do not shoot. Remain perfectly still while your partner walks off the field. Your opponents may or may not know where you are…let them think that the player walking off the field was alone when they spotted and shot him. Even when your opponents know you are there, they will often give up on scrutinizing the forest for "that other guy" when they see and hear no trace of you for a few minutes.

Add to this the problems that their goggles will often be foggy, that it is difficult to tell the difference between a perfectly still player and a clump of brush through thick forestland, and that many inexperienced players are more concerned with getting to the action than maintaining careful defense, and you will often get away with "disappearing." Wait at least one minute after you believe they gave up on you, and then move like a ghost towards their complacent flanks.

Walk backwards if you penetrate the skirmish line alone. Many players fail to notice armbands or hopper covers, and rely on their "instincts" to tell if a player is friend or foe. This leads to a lot of blue-on-blue, or friendly-fire, situations! But you can use this natural human tendency to your advantage when you find yourself behind enemy lines! Walk backwards, or in a manner that suggests you are fleeing from an aggressor.

When your opponents see you facing the same direction as they are, or fleeing from "opponents" that are in the same direction as their opponents, they will often wrongly believe that you are on their team. They will thus presume you to be harmless. Show them the error of their ways.

Charge!

For more woodsball strategies, see the *Maneuvers* section of the Tactics chapter!

SPEEDBALL

Out of the woods and all grown up, speedball is the most common style played in tournaments around the world. Gone are the trees that shade woodsball players, and very little—usually no—undergrowth is permitted between the manmade bunkers. Professional league speedball fields use artificial turf instead of dirt, and players from walk-on to pro use inflatable bunkers for cover. Fields are made from flat, open surfaces and the accumulation of anything rigid enough to stop a paintball: plastic, plywood, irrigation pipe ("Hyperball"), but mainly, inflatable bunkers. Players looking for fast action enjoy the pace of five minute speedball games, and tournament promoters appreciate using inflatable bunkers and portable netting to erect fields anywhere they find an open, level surface.

Paintball began in the woods with oil-based paint shot from pump action markers powered by 12gram disposable CO_2 cartridges. Now there is no paint in paintballs, semiautomatic markers can rip more than twenty balls per second and high-tech regulators meter out doses of compressed air from tanks that hold up to 5,000 psi. The technology grew at a staggering rate, and so too did the pace: players came out of the woods to play smaller fields with fewer people and shorter time limits. Speedball has not replaced woodsball, but rather evolved into its own unique beast. While scenario games took over the forest, speedball fostered the tournament scene. Now tourneys are synonymous with speedball, as scenario games are synonymous with woodsball.

Much of speedball's allure comes from having a high-visibility nature: it showcases flashy markers and jerseys and field designs that attract spectators. Bold moves impress friends lounging on the other side of safety netting, and crowds in the bleachers can cheer for their favorite teams. Since speedball games can be videotaped easily, and offer very engaging footage, there is a growing market for DVD's that chronicle professional games. Sports television shows and news broadcasts are increasingly mentioning and even featuring paintball, and it is speedball that rules the airwaves. Viewers who do not understand our sport can watch from the sidelines, or overhead, as a game unfolds before them on the television…and teams can use this resource to study the strategies used in pro games.

Paintball is considered an "extreme sport," as showcased best, perhaps, on speedball fields. With hunting and many other shooting-related sports disappearing slowly from our national conscience, new players are increasingly drawn more to the flash of speedball than the camouflage and patience of woodsball. They are drawn also to the straightforward game formats speedball offers: center flag, elimination, and the classic "capture the flag." Groups can play quick games of elimination, where the idea is to eliminate every one of your opponents with disregard for flags, since speedball uses smaller fields with fewer places to hide than in woodsball. The center flag format used in most tournaments is easy for audiences to understand, as the goal is to move the flag to the opposite end of the field. New scoring, based on either hanging the flag or not, with ties decided by eliminations, are also easy for even lay-spectators to understand.

Speedball is all about angles, strategy, and as the name implies: speed. Instead of ambushes, speedball players have the dreaded "bunkering move," and instead of stalking, they have "ghost walking." Top players snapshoot, a skill largely unique to speedball. They also look for the change in angles that a shift in position makes, such as giving them a tiny view of an opponent's ankle. The subtleties of precision shooting and minute changes of angle are checked by the ferocious game pace. The geometry of changing an angle to see a target is drastically altered when the target moves, as frequently they do. Small fields keep wide-sweeping flanking maneuvers in check, and the open ground between bunkers makes "ghosting" something of an art form.

The arms race in marker technology began when players modified the first pumps to cycle more smoothly. The spirit of technological one-upmanship broke into a frenzied sprint with the advent of electronic marker systems. Solenoids and finely tuned pneumatics allowed cyclic rates to jump above fifteen, then twenty, balls per second...and they show little sign of slowing down. New force-feed hoppers keep up with insane cyclic rates well beyond the 15 bps limit most fields—and tournaments—impose. Electronic fire control modes include burst, bounce, rebound, and an array of impressive settings, most of which—beyond simple semi-automatic-only—are not allowed at fields. So despite fields limiting rates of fire and fire control modes, the technology keeps striving for faster rates—and they put this technology in markers designed for speedball.

High rates of fire come in handy when players need to suppress a bunker while their teammates move, and for overcoming the growing lack of marksmanship new players display. Spraying and praying and its many derivations are often employed in tournaments to protect players in transit and to distract opponents. To keep up with rate of fire capabilities, new technology was developed in compressed air systems, gas regulation systems, and hopper feeding systems. Many of the technological advances in the last ten years have come about in developing speedball-specific gear.

Every three years your computer becomes outdated by newer, faster, and better technology. Every few years paintball sees "the next great thing," from semiautomatic markers, to speedball, to electronic markers, to inflatable bunkers. What comes next we can only imagine, and prepare for by practicing every chance we get…and that isn't so bad!

Arrange all of your gear in a lockable, separate room the day before playing. Go through everything you intend to take, clean anything that is dirty, and buy any supplies you need before the event. Then lock the room to keep children and pets out, and get some sleep. When you transfer everything to your car the next morning, double check that all the necessary gear is present: marker, goggles, pods and harnesses, squeegee, toolkit, backup marker, water, snacks, etc. Avoid leaving your gear in your car overnight, as cold and hot temperatures can harm paint and electronics…and theft is a universal concern.

Standard equipment for a tournament player includes a marker, hopper, air source, game timer, squeegee, pads and goggles. Most players also carry a harness with at least one, or as many as fourteen, pods of paint. Pods can carry around one hundred paintballs, or around one hundred forty paintballs, depending on the type of tube. They come in an almost infinite variety of colors and lid-closure types. Players carry squeegees, sometimes a battle swab, and often times wear an athletic cup and kneepads. More than this is generally not worn, or carried, onto the field, and tournament rules prohibit carrying velocity adjustment tools (hex keys) on the field.

Carry your squeegee in a comfortable and accessible position so that you can get at it quickly. Some pro players put their squeegees on lanyards and hang them from their necks, but the author eschews this method because it poses a choking and goggle dislodging danger. These players often put the squeegee on their backs, and risk dislodging their goggles when they remove the squeegee over their heads or swing it forward for use.

Carry your squeegee securely and safely with a lanyard and a belt loop. Secure the squeegee to the lanyard, then pull a few inches of lanyard loop through a belt loop. Now pass the squeegee through this loop, and pull it tight. The squeegee is now attached to your body, but dangling freely. Secure it by using a leg-mounted squeegee holder, or tuck it into the elastic bands on your kneepads. Either of these methods will work independently, but tying your squeegee to your body keeps you from losing it during a game.

Other options include purchasing a tank cover that has a built-in squeegee holder, or making a squeegee sleeve by taping a short length of PVC pipe to your tank cover.

Standard staging area gear for a tournament player includes a toolbox with screwdrivers and pliers, extra batteries, paper towels, marker oil, o-rings, extra squeegees, Loctite and Teflon tape, crescent wrenches, goggle defogger, a lens rag, extra pods, a light snack, and water. Luxuries include a backup marker, backup goggles, clean socks and dry shoes in case it rains or you end up running through puddles, a portable canopy for shade, and a personal Swedish masseuse.

Know about discard-able equipment. This equipment can be thrown, dropped, or otherwise leave your possession during the game and not result in your immediate elimination. If you leave your marker in a bunker and run off for the flag, you are usually eliminated after three steps. However, an empty pod can be dropped, thrown, or otherwise discarded without penalty. Squeegees are generally discard-able as well, though seldom are kneepads and other gear. Know before you play so that you can keep track of the gear you must keep on you!

Throw discard-able equipment clear of where you are playing. If a discarded pod is near your foot and takes a hit, a referee might erroneously call you eliminated for having a hit on your gear even though you discarded it. Throw the pod well clear of your position, usually towards the nearest tapeline, so that an erroneous call won't get you in trouble! This also helps to keep empty pods out from underfoot so you don't step on them.

Use a game timer to know exactly how much of your game is left. Seven minutes seems like a short time for a 5-man game, but you'll lose all track of time once that horn blows. A game timer will tell you when there are only a few seconds to do something brave before the time runs out.

You can better judge risky moves and important pushes when you know how much time is left. In games with points for the first pull, you can gauge the risk of making a mad dash for the flag when there are only seconds left: if you are eliminated, there is no time for them to exploit your team's new weakness and get the flag. But, if you get it, you secure the points. Group pushes in the final seconds are desperate measures normally aimed at securing first pull points, but the key is scheduling: you only know it's the last seconds of the game by having a timer to check!

Players who wear a talking timer strapped to their goggles, or in other places where they rely on the timer's auditory signals instead of reading the countdown, generally set their game timers for thirty seconds less than the maximum game time. When they hear the timer's warning, they know there are only thirty seconds left to finish the game!

Use game timers to keep track of the remaining time and orchestrate last-second moves

Arrive early. Beat the lines at the chrono stations, purchase your paint early, and enjoy the extra time to fix small problems and pod up in peace.

Walk around in the gear you intend to play in. Two days before the game, walk around for a few hours wearing all the gear you intend to wear on the field: pants, jersey, camo, pack, shoes, full pods (fill them with anything heavy to simulate paint), athletic cup, kneepads…As you walk, feel for anything that rubs annoyingly, is painful when you bend or run, chafes or gets in your way. Fix these problems, or use the experience to learn to deal with uncomfortable ordeals (like athletic cups). Make your outfit as light as possible, while still suited to the conditions. Fix the nagging little things before the chaos on game day!

Work on gear in the days leading up to the event, so that once your pods are full and your team is registered you have few worries the morning of the event. There is never enough time to get ready in the morning…unless you get ready the day before, and all you have to do is unpack the car and walk the field!

Walk the fields as soon as you are allowed. Start at one flag station, and walk to the first bunker you think wise to occupy. Count the paces, continuously looking towards the opposing start station and watching as angles between and around bunkers change. Look for "lanes," straight paths between bunkers that provide unobstructed corridors to other positions on the field. You are vulnerable any time you cross a lane, but so are your opponents!

Look out from each side of your first bunker and take note of which sides of what opposing bunkers you see. If you can see a bunker, then you can shoot it—but someone there can also shoot you. Take note of how tightly you must tuck into a bunker to be completely shielded from the opposing bunkers, and what positions offer better angles. With a bit of skill and practice you can drop shots over bunkers, so take note of bunkers to the rear of the field that you can lob shots over.

Repeat this for each bunker you plan to use as you advance to their side of the field, remembering your role: back player, mid-player, or front player. Pay attention to lanes, especially those that offer views of the entrances to snakes, large bunker structures on the fifty yard line, or key positions.

Walk from each start station to the first, then second, bunkers of every other player on your team, noting angles and where threats can come from. If a certain bunker is exceptionally vulnerable to an opponent in a corresponding bunker, remember that threatening bunker and keep opponents out of it with coordinated teamwork and heavy suppressive fire. This advanced thinking keeps your teammates in the game longer—and helps them keep you in the game longer too!

Reverse sides, and walk the other side of the field. You seldom know for sure which side of the field you will start on, and it is imperative that you understand what your opposition has to work with. When you evaluate the field from both sides you can predict where they are likely to put players, and you can identify their key bunkers. Understand them, and then destroy them.

Adapting to bunkers. There is a refreshing variety of bunkers in the world, from hard plastic bunkers to inflatable ones, stick piles to plywood. You can push into the inflatable bunkers like they are big pillows, or lean solidly against a plywood upright. Adapting yourself to the dimensions and styles of these bunkers is a challenge even seasoned veterans face as they go from plastic to wood to concrete bunkers.

Size up a bunker by looking at its general shape. Does it provide side protection, or just frontal protection? Can you stand up behind it, kneel down, or must you lie down? Will the balls break on it or bounce off? Can opponents see you through netting or Plexiglas? Can you slide into it without hurting yourself?

Bunkers that you can stand behind are generally called standups, or standup bunkers. These offer the greatest range of tactical options, as you may snapshoot while standing up, kneeling, crouching, or (to a lesser extent) lying on the ground.

Inflatable bunkers provide a unique tactical experience: balls can bounce off of them, there are often "holes" between the edges of adjoining bunkers, and the wind (and you!) can move the bunkers around in place. Practice on inflatable fields as much as you can before any tournament on an inflatable field, as they play differently from other bunkers and are the top choice for large tournament circuits!

Shoot unsuspecting players through the gaps between bunkers

Your team tactician should be a player with good spatial skills and knowledge of tactics. Have him study football strategies, professional paintball games on DVD, and any paintball strategy articles you run across in industry magazines. Turn to him for inspiration on first bunkers, special moves, and how to approach tight races in the finals.

Make a map while teams are allowed to walk the fields before the tourney starts, or download field layout diagrams from the tourney's website. Your team tactician should do this, and everyone needs to strategize with it between games. Graph paper works marvelously well for making small maps like these, or overlays to figure distance for downloaded diagrams, and gives you standard units of measure. A good rule of thumb is that each square represents a certain number of running steps.

Use normal walking strides to measure the width of and distances between bunkers. Pace off the field and decide on a scale for your map, then mark the boundaries on the paper with a dark marker. These lines become the tapelines, and next you indicate with an arrow and a cardinal direction (or landmark reference) which end of the field is which. Pace off the location of the start stations relative to one side-tapeline and the rear of the field. Work out-to-in to set the bunkers on the paper, drawing all of the bunkers closest to the tapeline before working inwards. Draw bunkers with a pencil, orienting them exactly as they appear on the field. As a final step, trace all the bunkers with black ink. This is your map, and should serve you well.

The most effective way of using this map is to purchase a clipboard, clear transparency sheets (the plastic overhead projector sheets used in schools), and dry-erase markers in blue, red, green, and black. Clip the map to the clipboard with one transparency sheet over it, and then draw a play onto the sheet with the markers. You can use one color to represent each team, or one color to represent the "opponents," and then individual colors for each of your teammates.

Beginning at your start station, trace the paths of each player to their first bunker. Trace your fictitious opponents' likely paths to their first bunkers, either based upon logic or what you see in games that day. Look at the angles provided to every player: which bunkers appear to be "key," and which lanes to shoot down to clip opponents when they move. Plot second bunkers, then third bunkers, and trace the game all the way to its logical conclusion. Use X's to mark where you anticipate eliminating opponents, large dots where you anticipate your players will stop to shoot, etc.

Orient the transparency to the field by drawing an arrow on the graph paper, and then tracing that arrow on the transparency. When you line them up later, the moves will exactly correlate to the bunkers. Switch the transparency films, and plan another strategy.

Blue bunkers are first bunkers, red bunkers are second bunkers; blue yardage markers show defensive positions, red yardage markers show offensive positions

Use these sheets to plan alternate plays, man-down strategies so your teammates know what to do when you lose players from different places, and how to counter different plays: such as completely stacking one side of the field (immediately flood the open side, switching the axis of play to the width instead of the length of the field, and running a front player right past their start station to backdoor the cluster). Use your imagination, but more importantly, watch other teams play and plot where their players go. Map games completely from start to finish, and look at where the winning teams put players off the break, where their second bunkers were, etc. Map shooting lanes and crossfire situations with dotted lines of a different color so you know where balls can go from players in specific places.

Be sneaky and creative when you plan a strategy, and base it on what has already worked mixed with radical ideas no one has tried yet. As you gain a feel for the field by watching others discover problems for you, such as cans not providing adequate side-protection from a player crawling down the snake, catalogue the lessons on your map to share with teammates and remember them when you take the field! After a while the teams will fall into a standard dispersal and use only slight variations of the same tactics over and over. Learn these tactics, and when it comes your turn to play, vow to not play the same strategies the other teams use…your opponents will be taken completely off guard!

If every team faces opponents who use variations of the snake-push stacking tactic, they will expect (and be able to counter) that exact move game after game. Change your strategy to something completely different, such as a wedge formation where you push past the flag and then hammer the tapelines from the center. Use the element of surprise by playing against their assumption that you will play just like any other team. When playing the same team twice, use different tactics each time.

Velocity limits vary from event to event and field to field, with the speed limit of 300 fps the general rule for tournament play. Know what the speed limit is for your tournament, and tell every member of your team. Chronograph often, especially if you play with CO_2. A hot marker penalty will cost your team undue points, and bunkering a player with a hot marker is just not cool.

CO_2 has a high boiling point, for a gas, and the curious property that it cools as it changes volume (like when it flows from your tank through your marker). As it cools, it becomes denser, and produces less pressure. On cold mornings, it takes slightly more CO_2 to achieve a given speed (say, 300fps) than it does later in the day when it warms up ten or twenty degrees. Now the same volume of gas will have a higher pressure, resulting in velocities that exceed the speed limit...even though you may not have touched the velocity adjustments at all. We have to chronograph repeatedly throughout the day to counter these fluctuations to avoid hot marker penalties and unsafe playing conditions.

Get a schedule as soon as possible, and highlight your games. Plan your air fills and pod filling so that your tanks and paintballs sit less than an hour before you take them onto the field. Air has a bad habit of leaking when you can least afford it, and paintballs can stick together in high humidity or otherwise perform below par if exposed to the elements too long. Be sure to leave enough time to get through the air lines and fill the pods before the game though; finding this balance is part of learning to be a master tourney player!

Watch the first games of the tournament, and then watch as many thereafter as you can. This should be a team event, leaving only one person to watch over your gear in the staging area. Watch which bunkers each team takes off the break, and how far each player runs before taking paint. Pay close attention to players in the bunkers you intend to occupy, and watch where they take paint from and who they can shoot at. Watch both teams equally.

Is the snake as important as it first seemed? Are your back players' intended first bunkers actually too far back to be in the game? Do the bunkers align to cover a sprinter on his way to the flag off the break? Make careful note of how the winning team accomplished their goal, and where each player on both sides was eliminated…and where they were shot from.

Stack the start station to keep players from tripping over each other. Most tournaments require players to start the game by facing away from the field, often with the barrel of their marker touching a banner or pole. This is to give the players an extra second to break out of the start station before taking paint so they actually have a chance at making their first bunkers. It also keeps teams from spreading out sideways or deep to gain unfair distance advantages to lanes and bunkers.

When your team fills the start station, put your tape runners on the "outside" of the cluster. Tape runners should always be given the outside-most positions so that they do not have to run past, in front of, or through any other player. Your mid-players go next in line on each side, followed by your back players. This is the basic way of stacking the start station. Players who turn and shoot should be the inside-most players in the stack so that no one runs in front of them. A player who is sent straight up the middle should be placed in the center of the pack so that he can simply turn and run straight to this bunker between the lane shooters.

Blocking balls from hitting your goggles by holding your hand in front of them is a popular off-the-break tactic for many pros. A paintball is more likely to bounce off of a hand than the hard plastic in goggles, so some pro players hold their weak hand up between their lens and the open field to deflect any incoming paint while they charge to their first bunkers. Turning your head away from the field also hides your goggles, but you lose the ability to watch where your opponents run.

Communication is critical, and involves every player's active participation. Back players are the primary talkers on the field, followed by mid and then front players, but everyone should echo a kill-count call or the location of a key opponent. Every player who sees an opponent move should call out that their opponent advanced, and more importantly, where he went. Agree on terms for the bunkers before the game: taco, can, snake, barrel, home plate, etc. The easiest names to remember are correlated to the appearance of the bunkers, and often use the color of the bunker as well. "Their thirty, blue taco, on me!" means that the blue triangular shaped bunker about ninety feet up from their start station is shooting at the player yelling.

Their thirty, our forty, my mirror, my cross field mirror, left tapeline…these are locations that help your teammates zero in on a particular bunker. When combined, "their thirty can!" first directs your teammates' attention to a location on the field, and then to a specific point on that plane. "Over there, dude!" means nothing to anyone. Silence means even less. When everyone agrees to use the same terms for certain bunkers, you all know exactly which bunkers are being talked about.

As important as calling out locations of opponents, players need to call out how many opponents are left, and also how many are still playing on your own team. Front players do not usually realize their team lost a back player or two until they need cover fire and can't get any; this is a bad time to learn you're down key players. Keeping an accurate handle on how many players your team boasts helps everyone refine their strategy and play style: your gutsy push becomes a suicide run with no back and mid players for cover fire support!

Game time occasionally expires while players search for a phantom opponent they think is lying in ambush somewhere on the field. Counting the dead box is a great way to avoid such problems. Screaming "splash one!" tells your teammates that an opponent was just eliminated, and "thirty two!" can mean three opponents are gone, but so are two of your teammates. The codes for eliminated opponents and players remaining on your own team vary widely, so design your own code that works well to keep track of the action!

Settle on a canon of code words for bunkers, opponent movements, and coming moves. Screaming your intention to bunker a player only tips him off that danger is approaching. Instead, come up with a short codeword or phrase like "flush!" to signal that specific move. Every player, from front players to alternates who sit out most games, should know each of your team's code words and what they mean.

Designate players to take care of specific tasks between games, like appointing one player to keep track of the schedule and know at all times how long until your team is expected to play again. Everyone should take care of their own gear, but one player can be designated as the pod filler, another one the designated schedule keeper, and another, the tactician. By assigning specific jobs, you ensure everything important is covered.

Rotate your paint from game to game, which means shooting the "older" paint first and "fresher" paint last. Running strains the paint in your pods by shaking the balls into each other and the side of the tube. Direct sunlight and heat are bad for paintball shell integrity—pod paint is exposed to both. Rotating paint helps you shoot your paint before any one pod is exposed to excessive bouncing, heat, or sun. When it is time to reload your hopper before the next game, reload it from a pod in your harness. Move the pods around so that the first pods you pull are the "oldest" paint that day, and put "fresh" paint in the tubes that you pull last. This will keep in-pod-breaks to a minimum, and help reduce barrel breaks!

Use your barrel plug or bag as a reminder to turn on your motorized loader. Barrel blocking devices do not need to be removed until you are at the starting station and just about ready for the ref to begin the countdown. They are inserted immediately upon being tagged. You only need to have your hopper turned on when your barrel plug is out, so use your plug as an indicator of when to turn the hopper on and off. If you frequently forget to flip the switch on your hopper, write "hopper on" on each side of your barrel bag. This will help you stretch the number of games you can get on one set of batteries, extend the life of the hopper's electronics, and prevent feed interruptions from rapid shooting with your hopper accidentally turned off!

Be ready for back-to-back games. Prepare before the first game by filling reserve air tanks and extra pods, and making sure your backup goggle system is clean and ready for immediate use. Take a bottle of water to the field, and drop it in the shade by the entrance to the netted area so you can drink between games without having to run all the way back to the staging area.

On your way to the field for the first back-to-back game, drop off your backup goggles, air, and paint in the shade by the entrance to the field. Have one of your alternate players or trusted friends stand guard over the stash.

Listen to the impact of the balls on your bunker, and do not fear them. Each ball you hear hit your bunker has just destroyed itself, and is no longer a threat to you...so the rumbling is not a sound of imminent doom, so much as the reassuring sound that your bunker is protecting you as it should.

Learn how to shoot with your weak hand, and open up a whole new side of the field!

Listen to which side of your bunker they are hitting, and snap out of the opposite side. When you know the opponent is focusing on the right side of your bunker, snap left. The instant you hear the balls cease pounding on your bunker, snapshoot from a different part of the bunker (high left, low right, etc.) and duck back in. Do not time your snapshooting to the sound of their markers: it takes a second for paintballs to reach you, so there is still paint in the air just after their shooting stops. Time your snap by the sound of the balls impacting your bunker.

Learn to shoot weak-handed. You should be able to shoot ambidextrously. Practice until you are as efficient with your weak hand as with your strong hand. This helps you play tight bunkers by shooting accurately from both sides. It keeps your opponent guessing, and opens up some of the best angles on the field.

Start training to shoot weak handed by going through the motions of shooting with your dominant hand. Slowly go through the actions of raising your marker to bear, sighting down the barrel or with a red dot scope, squeezing the trigger, watching the balls, adjusting your aim, and snapping back behind cover. Now, apply those exact motions to shooting with your weak hand. Pay attention to every detail and replicate it with your weak side.

For right handed players, grip your marker with your left hand and put your right foot towards your "opponent," a target erected for this exercise. Raise your marker to your left shoulder, aiming at the level of the target, and adjust your body to a comfortable position. Wrap your right hand around the expansion chamber, or wherever you normally wrap your left hand, and snap out from the bunker. Shoot three shots as fast as you can, and watch them fly towards the target. Once they hit, adjust your point of aim, shoot three more shots, and snap back behind cover. Repeat this sequence until you get the "feel" of the position and can keep a majority of your shots on target.

Now switch back to strong hand shooting for a few shots and pay attention to the subtle feel of shooting normally. Go back and forth between strong and weak hand shooting, making each feel as natural as the other. Pay close attention to foot position and keeping your body tight to your bunker.

Some players try to shoot weak handed with their marker secured to their strong side shoulder. This results in awkward positions, decreased accuracy, and the player needlessly exposing much of his body. Feel each movement in shooting correctly, and apply what works back and forth between the positions. Kneel or squat and repeat these drills to get the feel of shooting weak handed in awkward orientations.

Cross-up for defensive and offensive scenarios. When your team drops to you and one other player, "cross up" your streams of paint to protect each other and your flag station. Fall back to a position behind a solid bunker that provides frontal protection, and is flush against a tapeline so that no one can flank you. Have the other player do likewise, and then you each shoot out of your bunkers at the opposing tapeline.

The effect is to create a large X on the field with your streams of paint. Maintain that X by posting and sustaining an unpredictable rhythm of fire. Any player trying to bunker you must go around the front of your bunker, right into your stream. To even get that far, he must get past the down-range impacts of your partner's stream. Any player trying to run up the middle between you and your partner will be eliminated in the crossfire.

As an offensive tactic, have your front players on the tape cross up their streams in this manner and push forward under the cover of mid and back field players. Their sweeping streams of paint should lead to the elimination of the opposing front center-field player, and put your front players in position to bunker their counterparts. Your players will not be able to advance through the crossed streams, so proper communication is essential when it comes time for a bunker move or run through.

Run-and-gun without ending up on your face! Stay on your feet by training yourself to shoot crossfield while running and gunning. Imagine a straight line between you and your destination. When you shoot to the left of that line, hold your marker in your right hand. Your body is now moving "forward," and your feet are automatically falling one in front of the other while you maintain a comfortable body position.

Shooting right handed to the right of that imaginary line points your left shoulder and hip towards your destination, and you end up running in a side shuffle. That slows you down, and makes you trip and fall. The same applies in reverse: shoot left handed when engaging a target to the right of your destination, and your body will naturally run forwards, and faster! Try it, and you will notice an increase in comfort that translates to better accuracy and faster speeds!

Keep your shoulders square to your target as you run-n-gun. This means that you should run in a comfortable position, one that provides solid support for holding your marker steady. The angle of your shoulders should be around 45-degrees relative to the plane between your starting position and their bunker…in other words, do not stand with your entire chest facing downfield in the classic police shooting stance. Find an angle that is comfortable and works while running, and from which you can provide solid support for your marker, as this increases accuracy.

Sweet spotting on the break is a great tactic to keep opponents out of key bunkers, and usually eliminate one or two immediately. This is normally a move for back players, but all players can sweet spot on the field from their respective positions. When you walk the field before the tourney, look for shooting lanes that offer glimpses of the leading edges of key bunkers, and those that intersect the paths of players running off the break.

When game time comes, your back players need to turn and run to these lanes, and then put a solid stream of paint on the leading edge of key bunkers or waist-high down the lanes opponents run through. This stream of paint should be maintained until all of the opponents are in their first bunkers. After the initial bursts down the lanes, your back players should walk quickly to their first bunkers while continuing to suppress the edges of key bunkers and shooting lanes.

Put every other, or every third, ball past the bunker's edge. If all you do is rumble the bunker, there is no ball traveling beside it that can actually tag the player. When the rumbling is not enough to deter them, you need those balls flying past the edges to catch them when they pop out or slide in.

When aiming to clip a runner, choose a lane that is at least four paces away from their bunker or the starting station. The player can move about four paces, depending on the length of the field and your starting posture (markers down facing away vs. markers up facing the field, and all the variations…), before your first shots reach their end of the field. Bear this in mind and pick a

501 PAINTBALL TIPS, TRICKS, AND TACTICS

lane they still must run across by the time your paint gets to their end of the field.

The velocity limit at most fields is 300fps. On a field that measures 150 feet between start stations, it will take a paintball half of a second to reach the other side. Add another half second to bring your marker to bear from the start horn, and you have one full second to run before any of their paintballs begin impacting your side of the field. Conversely, they have the same second before your paintballs reach them. During practice, have a teammate sprint from the start station towards each tapeline, and note how far he goes in one second. The next lane that he crosses is the first lane that you can, and must, suppress off of the break—otherwise your paintballs will arrive too late to do any good.

Shooting lanes is a variation of the sweet spotting tactic. Certain bunkers are key bunkers, or positions that offer angles on the flag, the snake, or an entire line of opposing bunkers. Controlling key bunkers is critical to winning the game, so players push hard to control them…usually sooner rather than later. When you walk the field before the game, look for lanes that connect one bunker to another across the field. When you play, get to a position that offers a good angle on the leading edge of a key bunker. You know a player is going to move into that bunker, and you know which direction he will come from, so shoot beside the leading edge of the key bunker to clip him when he tries to run behind it!

Players are inclined to move when their bunkers stop rumbling, and so long as you refrain from hitting the leading edge of his next bunker, he will likely have little idea that you are setting a trap for him. When the player moves, he has to run directly through your stream of paint to duck into this new bunker. So long as you keep the stream dense (with a high rate of fire) and accurate, you'll get him…and you keep a key bunker empty!

Use this tactic to set traps for players when they move to key bunkers, try to bunker your front players, or any time that you anticipate a player is just about to make a move. Keep the stream in the air, and let them run into it. Beware that this technique involves posting, and that exposes you to snapshooters!

Look for intersections between adjacent segments of bunkers, like where two inflatable tubes meet to form a snake. Many inflatable bunkers are rounded on the ends and leave triangular holes between abutted corners and the ground. You can hit a crawling player through these holes, and sometimes look through them to watch how many players crawl downfield.

Other bunkers may have cracks and spaces between or under them, such as when using Ballwall-style obstacles on hard ground: the feet on the bunkers hold the bunkers about an inch above the ground, and you can easily rain paint on opponents' feet through that gap. Netted bunkers get holes in the net, and plywood bunkers sometimes pull apart in key places. If you can shoot through a hole, do it.

Be wary of sticking your barrel through a hole in your bunker, or shooting through a hole in your own bunker in any way. Oftentimes fields will have rules saying that your "bunker" is a plane of space as much as a physical barrier, and sticking your muzzle through a hole in the netting or shooting through an unnatural crack between sections is good to get you eliminated. Check on this before you play, and remember: if unsure about these rules applying to your bunker, play safe. If unsure about these rules applying to an opponents' bunker, shoot him and then let the refs decide after he wears your paint!

Taking paint yet? If paintballs from opponents aren't splattering all around you, or yours aren't splattering around them, you're not in the action. Move up, look out of your bunker, or in some other way get into the game…you're not helping anyone by hanging out away from all the action!

Posting is a tactic whereby a player keeps his marker trained on an opponent or opposing bunker without ducking back into his own bunker or significantly altering his aim. This leaves the player vulnerable to being hit, but provides instant awareness of his opponents' movement. Players who post are ready to instantly put balls on their opponent. This tactic *is* the definition of tunnel vision, but there are times when posting is more useful than dangerous.

Back players, by virtue of their distance from the skirmish line, are generally better able to safely and effectively post than other players. Snapshooting is not as critical to them, as they are normally far enough away from their opponents to hear their shots, see their balls coming, and duck to avoid them. Front players generally should avoid posting, as it leaves them very vulnerable to taking hits, and because it fosters tunnel vision.

Avoid tunnel vision. Tunnel vision means focusing all your attention on one player, bunker, or part of a field, to the exclusion of what is going on everywhere else. Focusing intently on one player leaves you vulnerable to other players moving up on you undetected. You might have shots on two or three other opponents after bunkering their front player, so be aware of the changing angles during the entire move. While snapping against one player, watch for movement elsewhere on the field and be prepared to spin and engage a moving player before you snap back behind cover.

What's with all the paint all of a sudden? Something is definitely happening when your bunker gets pelted by multiple players instead of just the one nearest to you. Players prefer to move under heavy cover fire, so when your bunker receives more than the normal coating of paint, someone is likely moving around. Are they coming to bunker you? Watch the shadows around your bunker and listen for marker pops and paintball thumps to grow louder, a sign that a player shooting at you is coming closer.

While your bunker gets rumbled, call out your team's code for "they're shooting at me," so that your teammates know there are players exposing themselves downfield. They can use the opportunity to pick off opponents while the offensive line shoots at you, thus using your opponents' own tunnel vision against them. When only one player is engaging you, call out which player is shooting so your teammates can side-shoot him while he is exposed.

Keep totally behind cover while you reload, or while waiting to move, unless executing a tactical reload—shooting while dumping in more paint. Crouching or leaning outside of your bunker telegraphs your move to your opponents and they can expect the move and anticipate where you are going. Explode suddenly from behind your bunker so they have no warning of your move.

When peeking around the side of a bunker, keep your marker fully behind it unless you intend to shoot...otherwise you are offering more of a target to your opponents. As a general rule, you should never peek out of your bunker unless you are pointing a marker where you are looking, and are ready to shoot any opponents you see. Otherwise you risk being eliminated, or letting them know where you are, without much reward.

Bunkering is largely the domain of front players. This crowd-pleasing move entails a player running around the side of a bunker and shooting an opponent at pointblank range. The maneuver is risky, though hard to counter, and always results in the elimination of one of the two players (and often both). Consider a bunkering move to be a trade where you eliminate your opponent at the cost of eliminating yourself. If you stay in the game afterwards, consider yourself lucky, and keep playing!

Three keys to successful bunkering are: knowledge, of timing and opponent orientation; cover, the paintballs your teammates shoot to suppress your target; and speed. Your timing must be perfect to catch the other player unprepared, such as when he focuses on shooting at one of your teammates, reloads, or cowers under withering fire.

Pay attention to which side of the bunker he favors. Based on his past behavior and the degree to which you believe him ambidextrous, deduce where he will be aiming—right, or left—before you leave your bunker. Run around the opposite side of his bunker to shoot him in the back.

Cover fire is imperative, as you need to keep your target's head behind the bunker as long as possible so your bunker move retains the element of surprise. Yell your code for "cover my bunker move," and wait for your mid and back players to start pounding the opponent's bunker.

Note the streams of paint, and do not run through them! You can shoot your own cover fire if no one else is available, but smart players will know that you are running to bunker them when the sound of your marker grows louder...though seldom does this knowledge register in time to save them!

Speed: you need to get out of your bunker fast, run around their bunker before they know what is happening, shoot them before they can shoot you, and then duck back into a bunker before their teammates nail you. If there are other players to bunker, or other players you can side shoot after your bunker move, shoot them quickly! Plan second bunker moves and side shooting moves before you start the charge, so you are ready when the moment arrives.

Your path should take you around the edge of your bunker, and then straight at the middle of your opponent's bunker. This way they cannot as easily peek around and see you running, and they have to lean out to increasing degrees to shoot at you. Your mid-players should be able to pick them off if they lean far enough around their bunker to get a shot on you. If the cover fire works, the opponent will not be able to lean out at all to see you running directly at their bunker. At the last possible second before colliding with the bunker, veer to one side with your marker pointed to shoot at the player's belly button. Shoot the first part of the player that you see: ankle, pack, back, whatever.

Aim for their belly button, because their midsection is the largest part of their body (especially when they are wearing a pack). This will put your muzzle at shoulder height for a kneeling opponent, and your aim will still be on their body instead of over their head. If you have the luxury of picking a part of their body to shoot, go for a fleshy area like their back or shoulder. In practice, it is kind to shoot them in the pack where a pointblank paintball will not hurt. In a tournament, though, the player will continue playing, oblivious to the pack hit, and painfully eliminate you. The ref may or may not pull both of you, only him, or wipe his hit and pull just you.

When you shoot him on the body, though, he gets incontestable proof of being shot…and a painful message to get off the field now or more are coming from the same close range. This prevents the honest mistakes that lead to accidental playing on and the pain of pointblank overshooting.

Preventing a trade when you bunker is simple. Many players of dubious scruples or dishonorable inspiration believe it perfectly alright to spin on the player who bunkers them, shooting their opponent even after being obviously and fairly eliminated. In the flash of bunkering action, referees seldom get a clean view of who-shot-who-when, and seldom have the super-human perceptions to puzzle out what exactly happened. When both players wear paint, they often eliminate both players. It is unfair, but without time to argue or film footage to play back, it is the best they can do.

But you can prevent being eliminated by these cheaters! The moment you shoot the player, twist your upper body, marker, and face away from him. If he spins, he will only be able to hit your shoulders and back. If you have a window of opportunity to eliminate another opponent, take it before the ref can call you out; or, take the shot and then immediately (and respectfully) turn to the ref and talk to him about your status as "eliminated." An acute referee will see your move, see the hits on your back, and conclude that you could not bunker the player with your back turned to him! Thus, since your marks are on your back, he shot you after you were done eliminating him.

Should the referees not take notice of this, calmly explain to them what you did, and show them your hits. Be ready to duck immediately behind cover—have this quick exchange behind a bunker—because the commotion is going to catch the attention of the rest of your opponents! You are not neutral unless called neutral, so you can be eliminated by a dastardly opponent while you stand there talking to the ref!

If you do get hit, get out quick, or you'll definitely get bonus-balled!

Avoid getting bonus-balled during a bunkering move with cunning footwork. Your opponent's chest will be facing his bunker, which is behind you when you run past him during the move. When you come around the player's left side while he is shooting out of the right side, he has to pull back from the bunker, swing his marker across his chest while pivoting on his heels, and then shoot at you. This gives you enough time to turn your back as you do to prevent a trade call, and it also gives you enough time to make a ninety degree turn and run directly behind the player. Players cannot shoot directly behind themselves, and he will not be expecting to have to spin so far around to unfairly shoot you!

This counter move is simple: just make a ninety degree turn to run directly behind the player after eliminating him. The extra rotation he needs to make will buy you the fractions of a second for a ref to realize you are clean, and your opponent is eliminated. Determined cheaters sometimes spin around so violently that they fall over, which adds invaluable smack-down factor to the glory of your bunker move, and the ignominy of cheating!

About to get bunkered? Experienced professional front players develop an instinct where they know when they are about to get visited by an opponent. The rest of us have to use science and logic to protect ourselves. Look at the shadows while you wait at the start station. When the shadows fall towards your side of the field, you can watch the ground around the sides of your bunker for an approaching player's shadow. This alone is seldom enough warning to counter their move, but can be used to tell which side they are approaching from when other signs indicate you are in trouble.

Silence warns as much as increasing noise. Listen for anything out of the ordinary. Not many players lay their own cover fire, so if you trade paint with an opponent in front of you for a while and he suddenly goes quiet, there is likely a good reason: he is charging to bunker you, or reloading his hopper. Lean around your bunker, marker at the ready, and find out why he broke rhythm or changed behavior.

Growing noise is also a sign, as a player laying his own cover fire gives away his move when the popping of his marker gets louder as he closes on your bunker. The thumps from impacting paintballs may also grow slightly louder as they hit with increasing force from the closing distance. Also listen for your bunker to get rumbled by numerous opponents suppressing you…there is a good reason they are doing this, and you need to find out why!

Reverse bunker your opponents to eliminate them when they charge. Figure that they are intelligent and will swing around your bunker on the side you have not favored in a while. For right handed shooters, this means that they will likely run around the left side of your bunker. There are times when you simply cannot wrap far enough around the front of your bunker to shoot them on the run without getting tagged by another opponent. In these cases, set a trap.

Crouch down to be the smallest target possible, and post on the side you anticipate they will swing around. Now that you are ready, work on your body placement. Be ready for the split-second window you have, whenever it comes.

You can work the offensive by holding your marker in the most appropriate hand for the side of the bunker you expect them to rush (left hand for left side, even if that is your weak hand). Then, while crouched, walk backwards away from your bunker and watch the leading edge of the obstacle. If you take more than three steps without seeing a piece of your opponent, lean sharply to change your angle around the bunker. Shoot your opponent and lunge back behind cover. Keep your marker up in case he tries to play on.

When challenging a "simultaneous elimination" call, use *Action Pursuit Games* Editor Dan Reeve's favorite argument: "My barrel is longer, so my paintball got there first." Laugh if this actually works!

Watch out for the "dead man's walk," a sneaky tactic considered a dirty trick in most social circles. Players attempt a dead man's walk when they stand up from their bunkers and walk, usually along a tapeline, nonchalantly towards their opponents' side of the field. They attempt to look like eliminated players walking off the field, but they do not hold their markers above their heads, install their barrel bags, or indicate in any of the prescribed ways that they are eliminated. Once behind their opponents, they bring their markers to bear and shoot as many backs as they can see.

Become suspicious if you see an opponent walking towards your side of the field instead of towards the dead box on their own side. If the player does not indicate that he is eliminated as per the field or tournament rules, shoot him a single time just to be sure he is eliminated.

Cut down on getting bonus-balled in the rest of the game by quickly leaving your bunker. A famous referee once commented "in an ideal game, the eliminated player would simply vaporize as soon as he gets tagged." For the benefit of your team, as well as your own health and well-being, exit your bunker immediately after being tagged.

Gregarious players might keep trying to shoot you, so indicate that you are eliminated by holding your marker straight up from behind your bunker. Scream "hit!" once, or more if allowed (some tourney rules only permit you to say "hit," and at that, only once, or your team will get penalized), pause to let any airborne paint fly past, and then briskly walk to the nearest tapeline. Put your other hand on your head to further signal that you are eliminated, and do not walk towards your dead box until you are a few feet outside of the tapeline.

Not sure how many opponents are left? Try to count the "dead box" if you can see the players standing in it. Check that number against the number of players who started the game. For recreational speedball or woodsball games, when you play the "close" side of the field, relative to the staging area, you can count the opponents you see leaving the field to go to the staging area. Moves are better executed when you know how many opponents you face!

Stay in the action! Don't call yourself out just because you're out of paint or your marker is down. If you stay in, you can still serve as a spotter for your team, and as one more target to draw attention away from your teammates. You can even intentionally draw fire so that your buddies can take shots when your opponents lean out to shoot you.

Fold your arms in the dead box so that refs don't call a penalty, thinking that you're pointing out positions on the field.

Cheaters are known to use body language to communicate from the dead box to their teammates. Intelligent referees watch for such behavior. Don't point to remaining players for any reason, and stand as still as you can to prevent the refs from misinterpreting your fidgeting.

Duck completely behind the walls of the dead box if you can. You miss watching the action, but you make it harder for your opponents to count your dead box, which is good for your remaining players! Referees will also be less likely to penalize your team for trying to cheat through signaling to your teammates.

Be magnanimous in victory and humble in defeat

Overshooting definitions and their penalties vary from tourney to tourney. Overshooting is generally defined as having four or more breaks on your body and gear per barrel shooting at you. Thus, a player who has six breaks on him is not overshot if two opponents were shooting at him. If one opponent shot him all six times and the other one missed, there is still no overshooting penalty. Conversely, if the player is hit five times by the only player shooting at him, an overshooting penalty should be assessed.

The penalty is generally around twenty points. Bounces do not count towards overshooting penalties. Occasionally an overshooting penalty will be assessed for "malicious bunkering," where a player shoots an opponent pointblank several times but fewer than required for an "overshooting" penalty. Due to the close range of bunkering moves, the malicious overshooting penalty may be assessed for three breaks, or five breaks even if multiple barrels are shooting towards the player.

Know your score at all times, and where it puts you on the leader board. Towards the end of the preliminary rounds, you can plan your final games around your need for points: do you have to win each game, or do you just need the first pull points and a few eliminations? A team that consistently gets first pull points can often get into the finals ahead of teams that have hit-and-miss winning records, so know where you stand and how much you need to win. Now go get it!

Winter play often means indoor play for many of us, so keep in mind the special considerations of this format. You may be able to drop shots over the top of bunkers if you turn your velocity well slower than the field maximum. Shorter distances make arcing balls over bunkers more challenging, but a lower velocity may be the ticket if you like this fancy trick!

Match your footwear to the field. Combat boots are popular for woodsball players, but do not offer many practical benefits for speedball players. Soccer and football cleats work well on outdoor speedball fields, but remember to avoid metal spiked shoes when playing with inflatable bunkers. For indoor action, switch to a high quality indoor soccer shoe specifically designed for indoor turf.

FRONT PLAYERS

Front players grab the center flag and eventually get it to the opposing flag station. They are the first players to the opposing flag station in capture the flag format games. They establish a skirmish line, the point at which two teams have each moved as far forward as they can, and they shoot cross-field angles to eliminate other front players. When someone needs a good old fashioned bunkering, front players do it. Front players are identified by a lack of cumbersome equipment, generally shorter barrels to promote tighter play while snapshooting, light footwear, and light pads.

They must stay tight in their bunkers, and often find themselves huddled behind small bunkers in the middle of crossfires between their own mid and back players and the entire opposing team! Speed crawling, sliding and sprinting are vital skills they use to get right in the face of the opposition. They dart from bunker to bunker and slide behind cover, victory within their grasp!

Front players often cannot see much of the action on the field, in part because they focus on eliminating other front players and grabbing the flag, but largely because their bunkers take the most paint from opponents desperate to stop their relentless push to the fifty. Because of this limited visibility, they rely on mid-players and back players to call out opponent positions, kill counts, and to let them know when they are in danger of being bunkered.

Finding angles to eliminate opposing front players is one of their primary goals. Once they breach the offensive line, front players have to rush as far as they can into their opponents' territory. Paintball games happen at blinding speeds, and swift front players can advance several yards behind the remains of the opposing front line. Often, they can arrive at a solid offensive bunker before the rest of the opponents realize their line is breeched. These are golden moments for front players, as they look to the center of the field to side-shoot surprised opponents.

This intrusion divides the opposition's focus, creating opportunities for more front players to drop their targets. The invading player just needs to stay in the game, side shooting players as he is able to without being eliminated. A player pressured from the front as well as the side can only retreat to a small part of his bunker before exposing an ankle, leg, or his own flank. This is the bad-place-to-be-in that front players relentlessly put their opponents.

Bunkering is most often executed by front players. They muster their energy and courage to sprint straight at the opposition, exploding around the side of the opponent's bunker and shooting him pointblank. This tactic was reviewed earlier.

Playing front requires specialized gear, special amounts of courage, excessive energy, and more than a touch of insanity. Front players say it's the most fun position on the field!

Carry what you need. Front players seldom need more than a hopper and one pod. Two pods are considered the standard for most front players in common tournaments. National Professional Paintball League players, National X-Ball League players, and front players in other major leagues carry up to six pods, but even pro front players do not usually go through them all. Regular players benefit from carrying less paint so that they can run faster, play tighter, and slide more easily. Front players shoot very little compared to mid and back players, so they simply do not need to carry massive amounts of paint.

To determine how much paint you should carry, load up with at least four pods per game for two or three practice games with your tourney team. Play the format (3-, 5-, 7-, 10- man) that you most often compete in, and after each game see how many pods you went through. This is the number of pods you need to carry, and more will likely be unnecessary. Mid and back players can get away with carrying too much paint, but front players need to limit themselves to maintain their speed and diminutive target profiles. The more pods you have on your back, the larger your side profile, or your front profile if your harness puts the tubes at your side.

Another limiting factor on the amount of paintballs that you carry is the capacity of your air source. If you play with a 12oz CO_2 tank that only gets 600 shots per fill, and you have 200 balls in your hopper, it does not make sense to carry more than 400 paintballs (three 140 pods is stretching it) in your pack!

Special gear helps front players stay fast, play tight, and get to key bunkers. Kneepads, shin pads, and elbow pads are some of the pads that help front players to speed crawl over harsh terrain and slide, dive, and fall behind cover without getting hurt. Most of their game is spent on their knees, or in strange body positions, so comfortable kneepads are essential.

Front players also use harnesses that carry fewer pods, such as the ones that only have slots for two pods, and elastic expansion sleeves for a few more. These systems normally put the pods behind the player instead of facing them to the front like many scenario harnesses. The reason for putting the pods behind the player is to slim his front target profile when he snapshoots and runs.

Most of these harnesses are oriented to angle the pods down for a more ergonomic draw, and many feature elastic loops between the slots to hold additional pods without adding excessive width or bulk to the pack when the slots are not needed. The author successfully uses a 3+2 season after season, citing the ability to securely hold three tubes for normal play and the functional ability to hold five tubes for cross-over play at big games where trips to the staging area are infrequent and difficult.

New harness designs, frequently offer one more elastic

expansion slot than fixed material slots, so 3-pod harnesses have +4 capacity by hanging pods off of each end as well as nestling them between fixed slots. These offer even more versatility for front players who are occasionally impressed into mid or back roles, and don't want to buy a second pack.

"The Football" is another tube-carrying option for front players, and comes straight out of the paintball history books. These are made by unceremoniously duct taping two pods together, facing in opposite directions, with the mouth of each tube sticking out about an inch beyond the base of the adjacent tube. These are carried in the weak hand, and when both tubes are empty, discarded as one unit. As discard-able equipment only applies to empty pods, the football must be carried until empty. However, they can be set down in the bunker next to the player, so long as the player does not leave a full tube behind when he moves.

Shorter barrels are ideal for front players. Two identical paintballs shot at identical velocities and angles will travel identical distances regardless of the length of barrel that shoots them; this is a property of physics, bent only by imparting spin to affect kinetic energy. Shorter barrels have no decrease in range over longer ones.

Accuracy comes largely from the paint-to-barrel match and the effectiveness of porting to reduce turbulence in front of the paintball at the muzzle. Shorter barrels can still provide on-target accuracy and normal range while providing front players with more maneuverability when they play tightly.

Bringing a 16" barrel to bear behind a bunker requires the player to back his body farther away from the bunker, exposing it more greatly to side shots than if he only had to align an 8" barrel.

Drop forwards position the front of the inline-mounted air source from one to several inches forward of the grip frame. This alters the balance of the marker, and with proper adjustment can move the center of gravity to provide quick, responsive snapping without muzzle-heavy droop or tank-heavy sluggishness. They also help shorten the overall length of the marker so that players can tuck more tightly into their bunkers. Choose an 8 inch barrel over a 16 inch barrel, use a 4 inch drop forward, and you can configure a front player's marker to be a full foot shorter than a back player's marker! Tucking tightly, as with your shorter marker, is paramount to making yourself a hard target behind small bunkers on the skirmish line.

Snapshooting is a simple and very necessary skill for getting paint on your target without unduly exposing yourself. Though you can snapshoot from any position, including prone, start training in the kneeling position. Raise your marker to point at the elevation of your target, while still fully behind the bunker. Now lean out quickly, exposing only your marker and goggles, without moving your feet. Your marker is already at the proper elevation to hit your target, and is firmly in place against your shoulder; all you have to do is adjust the windage slightly, and shoot. Only shoot three balls, and then snap back behind cover.

Try to preserve your point of aim as you snap back behind your bunker, so keep your marker up and keep in mind where exactly you saw your target. Wait a second, and snap out again, and your marker should be almost perfectly aligned to put your first shot on target! Make minor corrections while shooting, and snap back in before your first ball hits your target. Listen for the impacts, and repeat.

Snapshooting is great for front players who have little time to align their sights, shoot steady streams of paint, or look around for their opponents. Mid-players can hang out a while longer to put more cover fire downrange for the front players to advance. Back players need not snap so much as post in a manner that presents the smallest target possible, but if your front lines fall, your back players will need to rely on snapshooting to survive!

Look for cross-field angles. This means that a front player on the left tape should look towards the right tape for opponents, and let the right tape player and midfield player worry about what is in front of him on his own boundary line. Consider the lane immediately in front of your bunker to be a "blind alley," a place you should not really concern yourself with. Trading head-on with a player directly in front of you rarely results in a quick and safe elimination, so let your cross field teammates side-shoot him while you focus on your own cross field angles. Good back players will keep you safe from being bunkered by anyone in this alley, and centerfield and opposite-tape players will eliminate anyone who is there.

Your job is to eliminate anyone in the blind alleys in front of your teammates. Looking for side angles like this helps break tunnel vision on "the guy in front of me." Shooting at this angle also gives you side shots on players, where they usually do not expect to be engaged. Few tourney bunkers give side protection, so once you pull tightly up to the skirmish line you will see all sorts of ankles and packs hanging out…and maybe a nice clean shoulder you can mark up!

MID PLAYERS

Mid players are jacks of all trades, capable of raining paint like a back player, or hustling to the skirmish line like a front player. They fill in gaps as they open, replacing a back player and covering his section of the field or sliding into the bunker a front player just left to plug the skirmish line. They are characterized by speed, a medium amount of pods in their harnesses, and loud voices. Back players and mid players control the action through communication, cover fire, and laning. While all players are responsible for communicating effectively, the mid players are especially important for tracking opponents' moves.

Teams usually have mid players in 7man and 10man formats, but never in 3man or 2man. All three players in 3man usually are impressed into "front player" tactics and positions by virtue of their lower numbers. 5man games have "back" and "front" players, and some strategies call for a "swing" player who acts like a mid player with a jackrabbit's speed.

Use your mid players to support a strong front line and fill in when players get dropped. Use your back players to support the mid players and long-ball the opponents. If this general concept is followed, there is no need to waste a player on "guarding the flag station."

Mid players fill in where they are needed: be it a tapeline position that opens, or for a back player who gets tagged. They also fill in when front players advance, and are the primary source of point-cover. Players often pick one or two opponents to cover, so when a front man is ready to move, the mid player needs to rain paint on the two players who are most likely to snapshoot the mover.

When securely in position, the mid player must decide between posting on specific threats or advancing to a more advantageous bunker. Often, front players move into positions as vulnerable to them as they are threatening to a specific opponent (standing even with and to the side of an opponent gives them a great full-body target, but usually involves running into the open to get it).

The moves that keep them in the game use surprise and quick shooting, but the extra seconds bought with the cover fire from their mid player is often the difference between a brilliant advance and a suicide move. Mid players need to rattle the bunkers of the most threatening players until their front player can eliminate them. When the front player can safely tuck behind his bunker and not be side-shot, then the mid player can think about moving up.

Moving up is best accomplished under the cover fire of a back player, and better yet when orchestrated with the timely snapshooting of front players. The mid player sometimes moves to the bunker formerly occupied by a front player, if it still yields advantageous angles on the opponents, or to another bunker that gives better angles or more direct views of remaining opponents.

Running the opponents' flag to your own start station is how you close the game in the NPPL, though many other formats currently use a center flag format and some even toy with the classic concept of total elimination. As front players relentlessly push the skirmish line farther back, mid players should be sure to take the center flag if their front line missed it.

When it comes time to sprint the length of a field to run your opponents' flag back to your station, mid players are generally the most prepared. Front players tire from all their sprinting, diving and crawling. Back players need to focus on covering the field in case of any surprises (which there should not be if you count the opponents' dead box), and are traditionally averse to flat out running.

BACK PLAYERS

Frequently maligned for slow movement and often referred to by their linebacker physiques, the modern back player is no longer the stereotype of a portly gentleman loaded with extra paint like a pack mule. They do characteristically carry more paint than any other player, and often play back by virtue of their tall (or wide) bodies not fitting well behind smaller forward bunkers, but the modern back player is evolving into a specimen as fit and mobile as anyone else on the field.

Back players first appear as easily identifiable figures in 5man, and are present in 7man, 10man, and open play as well.

Back players' primary jobs include fire support and communication. Back players rumble their opponents' bunkers, protecting their front and mid players. They get eliminations by sweet spotting off the break and laning during the game, dropping shots over distant bunkers and clipping the backs of careless players across the field. The cover they provide keeps their front players in the game by suppressing threats while the front players make bold moves.

Most back players shoot from standoff positions relatively far away from their opponents. This means that they engage most of their targets at cross field angles instead of head on. Though back players need to shoot cross field when they can, many of these angles are limited by intervening bunkers. Thus, good back players become experts at shooting blindly over intervening bunkers to drop shots on the opposition. Also, they often favor bunkers on the tapelines where they can find unobstructed views of snakes and other side-field bunker arrangements.

Players must communicate to effectively adapt their team strategy to the changing conditions of heated games. Front players need accurate coordinates to locate opponents, and updates on how many are left, because the job of eliminating these players falls largely to them. But, with the limited visibility of tucking into a bunker while multiple opponents mercilessly pin them, front players must be updated on the action by mid and back players.

With the back player role comes the power to control the movements of front and mid players—and this is where the back players come into their own as strategists. They command their opponents to stay down by shooting ceaseless streams into and around opposing bunkers, and they use booming voices to tell their teammates where to go and when to move. When the time comes for a bunker move, they yell a code to a particular front player and lay cover fire while he madly dashes forward. When the opponent walks off, they are the first to yell their code for "one more down," such as "splash four," to indicate how many opponents are still in the game.

Special gear helps back players keep the balls in the air and their opponents' heads down. Long barrels are popular on inflatable fields, with many back players choosing a two-piece barrel system with an eight or nine inch tip for an overall length of 14" to 18". These do not help the paintballs shoot farther, but come into play for sneaky tricks.

Back players press their barrels sideways into the inflatable bunkers, with the effect that the bunker wraps itself around the barrel and the marker moves a bit farther behind cover by virtue of shooting "through" the edge-plane of the bunker. Pushing hard sideways and wrapping the bunker around their barrel greatly protects their hoppers and results in a tighter playing profile. The longer the barrel, the deeper they can push the barrel and the more protection the trick affords.

Large capacity packs, carrying anywhere from two to fourteen pods, are a staple of back player gear. Their constant streams of paint drain hoppers and pods at a phenomenal rate, so carrying plenty of pods is vital. Larger capacity air tanks, such as 4,500 psi 114ci specimens, keep the markers powered steadily for hundreds of shots per game. They also carry a squeegee, like any other player, and are a bit more likely to use it by virtue of the amount of paint they shoot in a game. Electronic markers in general, and anti-chop eyes in specific, are blessings to back players.

Tactical reloads keep them in the game. The interruption in suppressive fire needed to fill a hopper is all the invitation many wily opponents need to bunker your teammates. While shooting steadily, draw a pod with your weak hand, open your hopper, open the tube, reach up and dump it in while not missing a beat with your trigger finger. You can stop just long enough to bounce your muzzle downwards to get the last of the balls out of the tube, and then throw the pod and slap the lid closed in one movement. This virtually eliminates the pause most players take to reload!

Arcing shots is effective to wrangle a bit of extra distance out of your paintballs. A master back player knows the exact trajectory of his paint, and can back up on his end of the field to adjust the distance to this target to lob paintballs over bunkers. This can clip players in the head. Mastering the arc shot takes time and talent, but with the right application of physics and enough practice you can make magic happen.

Advancing down the field is as vital to back players as anyone else. When the skirmish line pushes forward the back players should move up proportionally as soon as it is safe to do so. As they engage targets deeper in opposing territory, and need to protect their front players from increasingly close opponents, they benefit greatly from shortening the space between their muzzles and the opposing line.

During the end game, when the front and mid players sweep the field and run the flag in, the back players need to provide scanning cover in case of "surprises" and call out exactly how many players remain by counting the dead box and subtracting that number from the total number of players the team started with. One player hiding in a snake can devastate a complacent team in the end game unless a keen back player keeps them aware that someone still lurks in the shadows.

Is your flag runner clean? If your flag runner has a hit, even one they didn't feel, the hang won't count. Depending on the time remaining, and the individual rules, you may not get a chance to have a clean player hang it—you might just lose, or give the points to your opponents! Have one player check the flag runner, and if there is any suspicious amount of paint on them, change runners…making sure that the new runner is clean, too!

STRATEGIES

Consider your strategy. The basic 3-man plan is to run two players along the tape, one per side, and the third player up the middle. When two teams employ this same strategy simultaneously, a skirmish line forms that spans the width of the field. So, in tourneys where this happens to your team, "stack a side," by sending your middle player to one of the tapelines. Your tape players should "cross up" their streams of paint to make a giant X in midair. This will prevent your opponents from advancing while your middle player repositions to get an angle on their tape players.

Once you blow a tapeline, push your corresponding tapeline player into that hole and swing the skirmish line to box your opponents in against a side tapeline. Most bunkers only provide cover from the front, not the side, so you can make quick work of any remaining opponents if you push deep enough onto their side of the field while you move the skirmish line sideways!

Manipulate the angles on the field by repositioning your body. You know that a whole new world of angles opens up when you look cross field; even more open up when you move laterally! Once your team gets a player or two up you can make a few risky moves, such as standing in the open to get the perfect angle on a cowering opponent.

Imagine an overhead view of your opponent behind his bunker, with a big V drawn over him so that the point of the V is on his head and the legs intercept the edges of his bunker. You must be outside of that V before you can get a shot on him. Get there by swinging laterally, towards a tapeline instead of pushing closer to the skirmish line. Call for your team to suppress every player (you should have a call for "full suppress"), then quickly side-shuffle through the open field until you see an ankle, pack, or other part of the player. Shoot him, then duck behind the nearest bunker.

In this fashion you can eliminate a player without getting in his face, and often times bunker him with fewer of the problems of opponents spinning and playing on. This move is a hybrid of a bunkering move and a cross field angle shot, and works well at many distances!

Crawl. It's that simple. Pay attention to the height and align-ment of bunkers when you walk the field. Look for places where low bunkers combine with the rest of the obstacles to obscure one side of the field's view of the grass. You can find entire pathways across or up the field that completely hide crawling players!

Front players thrive on intensity!

Refine your low crawling at team practices. This is the on-your-belly version of ghost walking, a tactic for which Mike Paxson is infamous. Don your goggles, pack, and long pants, grab your marker and go get intimate with the dirt. Lay with your chest, stomach, and thighs flat to the ground, arms out in front of you. Drag your right knee up to your waist, plant your knee firmly against the ground, and then straighten your leg out to propel your body forward. Alternate knees, and keep your arms stretched in front of you.

For the most effective low crawl, lay your marker across your arms and turn your head to the side, letting the grass barely touch your goggles. This is a moving tactic, not an offensive posture, so do not worry about keeping your marker pointed towards threats or your finger near the trigger. Get into position first, then assume a tactical posture and destroy your opponents!

Ghost walking can take you clear up the field without detection or threat. Look for bunkers that align to obscure the opposing side's view of a certain area of the field. Two large bunkers that are slightly misaligned will block their view of a wide path. Add a third bunker just to the side of being inline, and the obscured corridor is even wider.

Notice how you can put a large bunker, say a big structure used as the flag station, between you and an opponent to completely obscure his view of your position. You have a large area to move around in without detection. The size of this area depends on the interaction of the size of the bunker between you and how far away you each are from it.

Think of an overhead view of your opponent and the intervening bunker. Imagine that large V again, drawing it with the point on his head and the legs clipping the sides of his bunker. As the player gets closer to the bunker, the legs of the V spread out as the bunker takes up more of his field of vision. As he retreats from it, the legs close in because the bunker occupies less of his field of vision. You are safe from detection so long as you stay between these lines. You must get outside of these lines, though, to have a shot at him.

When you add a second bunker to the equation, you see another spot that is safe from this player detecting you. If these safe places overlap, you have a corridor that you can move in with impunity. With that in mind, you can walk well away from the bunkers and still be protected by them. When you walk away from them, you change the angles that you see on the field. Change these angles to offer different views of other opponents, while remaining "hidden" from the opponent engaging you!

One opponent left? When there are two or more of you, take advantage of the manpower and swiftly deal with that last opponent. Have your buddy shoot the opponent's bunker, alternating left and right sides (and the top if the opponent can shoot over the bunker). Swing wide on your opponent…with your marker up! While he cowers from the suppressive fire, you should get a clean shot at a small piece of him. If not, shoot suppressive fire at him while charging in to do a classic "bunkering move." So long as the paint is flying his way, and not yours, you have the advantage!

TECHNICAL TIPS

MARKERS

Perform basic, routine maintenance on your marker to ensure proper function. This seems obvious, but some critical steps are often overlooked. Wiping the shell, fill, and black gunk from the inside of the marker is standard cleaning. Proper maintenance goes further, and involves inspecting all of the o-rings, inspecting the condition of parts in high-wear areas, and tightening loose screws. Inspect o-rings for nicks and abrasions, and replace them at the first sign of cuts, flat spots, discoloration, or other damage. O-ring kits that have all of the necessary o-rings for your particular marker are commonly available, and don't forget to check the o-ring on your tanks!

Keep an eye on damage to internal parts from sand or grit entering high-friction areas, such as between the bolt and the chamber, or dirt getting inside the valve. Routinely disassemble the valve at home in a sterile environment to clean the pieces and lightly oil them as recommended in the owner's manual. If you see signs of abnormal wear, such as scratches on the bolt or stripped threads on a screw you can't remember over-tightening, investigate immediately.

Damage is always a sign of a problem, and many problems you can solve by tightening or loosening screws, using the right lubricants, and removing grit. You may have to polish a bur or otherwise head off further damage, which is normally as simple as rubbing a jeweler's cloth or fine-grit sandpaper over the bur until you can no longer feel it with your fingers.

When working on your gear, keep your tools out of the mud and off the ground. Carry an old towel or drop cloth to set gear upon. Keep tools in your toolbox or on your table or tailgate so they stay clean and dry. Putting a towel down under your tools is a great help!

When working on your marker, work over a white cloth towel. Small pieces are easy to see against the white background, and the texture of the towel keeps them from rolling off the table. This also keeps the parts from picking up dust, dirt, sand, and other contaminants commonly found on work tables and in staging areas.

Lay the marker parts on your work towel in the orientation they are found in the marker. Imagine the marker resting on the towel, and with that as a guide, place the parts on the towel exactly where they would be inside the marker if it was laid back down. When you reassemble it, this will help you be sure of which bolts go where and what direction small pieces should face. Keep a parts diagram handy so that you know where all the pieces go if you get confused, and to order replacements for worn out or lost pieces. Many owners' manuals have exploded diagram views, and schematics can usually be found online.

Clean the ball detent every time you thoroughly clean your marker. Many ball detents are replaceable units that feature a nylon or stainless steel ball captured in a hollow bolt and kept under light pressure via a spring. Broken paint, excess oil, dirt, and other fouling material may accumulate around the ball and hinder performance. The result: barrel breaks near to your chamber, or accuracy reducing sidespin imparted to the paintball!

Determine what kind of ball detent you have by consulting the owner's manual, or by looking at the outside of your marker's chamber. Bolt heads that don't seem to be holding anything on, as on Autocockers, suggest you have a ball-style detent, while seeing a wire nubbin running along your marker and then disappearing into the chamber (as on Chipley Custom Machine markers) means you have the nubbin style detents. Tippmann and similar markers have a rubber nubbin that rests in a recess inside the chamber, and is removable during field stripping; make sure you put it back in the right way (with the point of the nubbin facing down the barrel).

For the types with a captive ball in a chamber, you may unscrew the entire unit from the body of your marker and submerge it in a glass of water. Using your fingers, pump the ball up and down in its track to cycle the water through the unit, removing any fouling inside. Shake it dry, towel it off, and add two drops of paintball marker oil, pumping the ball up and down several times to ensure that the oil spreads evenly throughout the unit and displaces as much of the water inside as possible. Wipe the ball clean, pump it again and wipe it a final time to remove excess, dirt-trapping oil. Reinstall carefully.

If this style of detent works itself loose while you're shooting, wrap the threads with two turns of Teflon tape (plumber's pipe sealant tape). If it seems to be protruding too far (i.e., giving you too many chamber-area barrel breaks), slip a thin o-ring all the way up the shaft, and then reinstall—the o-ring will keep it from threading so deeply into the chamber.

Other ball detent styles include the "nubbins" found in classic Automag designs, as well as rubber nipples and rubber pads (the latter as seen in many Tippmann markers). Simply wiping these pads with a damp cloth should be sufficient, and you should always be sure to reinstall them correctly. Pay attention to their orientation when you remove them, and reinstallation will be easy.

Rainy days are still good for paintball, if you prepare your marker properly. Water attacks the gelatin used in paintball shells, even cornstarch-based shells. Keep your paint dry by loading your hopper under a roof of some sort, and not opening your hopper in the rain unless you absolutely must.

Water in the barrel creates friction issues, which may well make your paint slip and spin in your barrel—and then curve mightily in flight. Keep your barrel dry by switching to a non-ported barrel that still offers a good ball-to-bore fit. If you must use a ported barrel, run strips of tape the length of your barrel, covering the holes. Secure each end of the tape to the barrel by wrapping more tape around the muzzle and the rear of the barrel. Duct tape leaves your barrel sticky, and masking tape often will not stick to the metal effectively enough to be useful, so try electrical tape!

Water also gets into your marker through the vent holes in power feeds, so you will need to construct a special flap from duct or electrical tape to cover this hole. If you simply tape over it, the excess air blowing back up the stack will travel through the power feed and bingo-ball your paint. This leads to slower rates of fire and increased chops. Not covering the hole leaves the paint exposed to rain, sleet, or snow.

Begin by cutting a three-inch strip of duct tape. On one corner of this strip, draw a 1 inch x 1 inch square. Cut that square out and discard it. Now, fold the sides of the flap together so the sticky sides touch, and you will have the flap, with a 1" strip of exposed sticky-side to affix the flap to your marker. Place the flap over the vent hole in the power feed, and if necessary, secure the flap in place with a band of electrical tape around the sticky part of the flap. It can now bounce to vent gas from the chamber and still keep the rain away from your paint.

Barrel shooting loose? Certain markers shake their barrels loose due to strong vibrations during cycling. This partial unthreading creates a gap between chamber and barrel that can lead to barrel breaks, and the misalignment and loose fit can greatly hinder accuracy.

To cure the problem, wrap two layers of Teflon tape around the threads on your barrel, then screw it into your marker. The tighter fit and increased friction between the barrel and marker will impede the unthreading.

If your barrel has a shoulder between the end of the threads and the body of the barrel, you can try the o-ring trick. Take just your barrel to a hardware store and find an o-ring that fits tightly around the shoulder of the barrel in front of the threads. Select an o-ring that is 1/16 of an inch wide, or narrower. Use this o-ring to act as a shock absorber between your barrel and the front face of your marker by sliding the o-ring up against the shoulder of the barrel and then threading it into your marker normally.

Look for other threaded pieces that come loose, such as the velocity adjustment bolt or the bolts that hold the grip panels on. Use a sparing amount of Loctite Blue on these threads to inhibit the effects of vibration and general use.

There are two types of barrel-related ball breaks: chops and barrel breaks. Knowing the difference will help you fix the problem, and help you more accurately tell a tech what is going wrong. A chop is when the bolt pinches the ball between the bolt face and the upper part of the chamber. A barrel break occurs when the paintball disintegrates somewhere in the barrel, but is not chopped in the chamber.

Chops occur when the rate of fire exceeds the rate at which the balls can completely enter the chamber, or when a paintball rolls partially back up the feed neck when the marker is held at an angle. This is sometimes caused when fill, oil, mud, or other residue in the feed tube slows the paintballs on their way to dropping into the chamber. Clean the feed tube on your marker, as well as the feed neck on your hopper. Check your rate of fire setting to ensure you are not shooting too fast for your given feed rate. Gravity, unaided, can effectively drop about fifteen balls into your chamber per second under ideal conditions. You may chop if you shoot at or around this rate of fire in any mode, semi or automatic.

To prevent chopping, invest in an agitated or force feed hopper. Paintballs in gravity feed hoppers often clog the feed neck so that you have to shake the hopper to get them to feed single-file. This slows you down, interrupts your rate of fire, and can lead to chops since the rhythm of paint feeding is uneven. Agitated loaders stir the paintballs so they do not bind at the mouth of the feed neck. Force-feed hoppers put a safe amount of pressure on the stack of balls feeding into your marker, so that gravity is assisted in keeping paint in line to shoot.

If your marker is at an angle when you shoot, the paintballs must roll to get into the chamber, which slows their descent and increases the likelihood of chopping. When all else fails, slow down your rate of fire.

Barrel breaks are easily prevented with regular inspection and light maintenance. Remove the barrel from the marker, and run water through it. Dry the barrel and remove the paint by pushing a dry patch (a 1 inch x 1 inch piece of cloth or paper towel) through on the end of a clean squeegee. Look through the chamber (not the muzzle). Inspect the bore for scratches, marks, or burs. Inspect the crown of the muzzle for burs that would snag a paintball, and if you see any damage, consider a new barrel. To fix a bur, you can purchase a jeweler's polishing cloth and smooth the rough spots yourself.

To fix a bur, wrap the jeweler's cloth around a wooden dowel rod (never insert metal into your barrel), and insert the cloth/rod until they are pressing against the bur. Now, spin the dowel rod to rub the cloth over the bur and smooth it out.

Factors inhibiting accuracy. All sorts of factors and phenomena conspire to degrade your accuracy, but there are things you can do to help make those balls fly like darts. Consistency of air pressure is a big one: notice how the chrono speed varies from shot to shot? Just as you expect a ball traveling 285 feet per second to go farther than a ball traveling 278 feet per second, they'll also have different flight paths and slightly different points of impact at a given range.

With a consistent burst of air coming out of your bolt each time, you'll have consistent velocities, and more consistent accuracy. Routinely cleaning your bolt, valve, and the internal surfaces of your marker will help stabilize velocity.

Paintballs are not perfectly round, no matter how good their quality—especially not after sitting for a few weeks or months, or being exposed to humid air and then let sit. Since they become, to varying degrees, of out-of-round, they will have varying flight paths. Generally the higher quality paint is more consistent than the bargain-box balls, and properly-stored, fresh paint will be far more consistent than paint improperly stored for a long time.

The fill settles over time, as most solutions naturally separate into strata after a while, affecting their center of gravity and destabilizing their flight paths; also, over time (and especially if exposed to humidity), they will develop dimples where other balls press against them, which alters their aerodynamics and can open up new places for air to slip around them in your barrel.

As your paint moves down the barrel, it's not going to fit perfectly. If it does, likely it will stick in places from the friction and burst in your barrel. So to get out of your barrel intact, there needs to be just a hint of space around your paintball—which opens up a world of necessary evil. The expanding gas pushing your ball wants to make it out of that muzzle as quickly as possible, and will slip around the ball wherever there is a gap. In extreme cases (as utilized by "Flatline" barrels) this will impart spin to your paintball, making it curve in flight. Thus, matching your paint to your barrel is crucial.

Ever watch the jets shoot water into a swimming pool? The water roils where the new water, under pressure, mixes with the existing water. The same thing happens with air at your muzzle: your paintball pushes the air in front of it away, out of the barrel, creating turbulence that it then has to fly through. Given that your ball will fly several dozen yards, even one degree of change in its direction will result in several inches—or several feet—of change in its impact point.

Use a ported barrel to reduce that turbulence, and improve your paintball's accuracy! They also quiet your shots a bit (sometimes dramatically), as your paintball won't "pop" out of the barrel with a sudden burst of gas behind it—rather, the gas vents through the ports, redirecting some of the sound and eliminating the "pop" part of the marker's report.

Get a barrel set. Having a wide selection of barrels in your gear bag, each with a different internal diameter, will help you match the day's paint to your barrel for optimum accuracy. Common bore diameters range from .684 to .693. Purchasing a barrel kit of different barrels, or different "barrel backs" (the rear of a two-piece barrel), specifically made for sizes in this range and labeled to that effect, is a popular way to cover the spectrum. These barrel kits usually offer interchangeable sleeves for the rear half of a two piece barrel, different back pieces, or occasionally complete barrels in each specified diameter.

Take a paintball from the case of your day's paint and insert it into the chamber end of one barrel. If the ball rolls all the way through, the fit is too loose, and the ball will bounce around inside the barrel as well as allow air to get around it. When air gets past the ball inside of the barrel, it swirls and creates turbulence in the bore and at the muzzle. This alters the ball's flight path and destroys accuracy. The fit is too tight when you have to push hard against the ball to get it into the barrel, and these tight fits generate too much friction for proper acceleration and paintball-safe pressures. Over-pressurizing the ball in the bore will make it burst!

The fit you seek is tight enough to keep the paintball from rolling out of the barrel, but loose enough that you can blow the paintball through the barrel, like a blowgun, with a moderate breath.

This match will yield optimal accuracy with best gas efficiency and the lowest likelihood of barrel breaks induced by too-tight-fits. Check the match again as the day wears on. Changing humidity and temperatures make the paintballs swell and shrink slightly, which affects the fit enough to warrant a different insert or back piece even though you can't see the change with your naked eye.

Barrel Breaks? Balls may explode in your barrel if the velocity is set too high. Remember that the international speed limit for paintball markers is 300 feet per second, and any velocity faster than that is unsafe to shoot at a person and likely to result in balls bursting in your barrel. Lower your velocity to the field speed limit, or a few fps slower.

Your bolt face may have burs that puncture or scratch the ball during cycling. Inspect the bolt face and replace the bolt if it's damaged, or smooth any burs with your jeweler's cloth.

Be sure the barrel is the right barrel for the marker, as even though the thread pitch might match, the throat length could be different. For example, you can use a Tippmann A-5 barrel in an

Inferno, but there is a 1/8 inch gap between the end of the chamber and the beginning of the barrel. Paintballs can bounce around in this opening, gouging themselves on the exposed lip of the barrel and bursting just in front of the chamber.

Bore-check your paint and be sure that you have a proper fit. Other factors that can induce ball breaks include ball detents that have burs, do not retract as they should, are unduly stiff, or project too far into the chamber. Old paint, as the shells change with age, is prone to breaking in your barrel, as well as paint that was exposed to water, left lying on the ground, or otherwise had its shell integrity compromised.

You must clean your barrel properly to avoid making a barrel break worse. Carry both a traditional squeegee and a battle swab when you play, and use each correctly. After breaking a ball, use the squeegee to remove the broken shell and fill. Push the patch-end on the straight shot, or push the squeegee head sideways on the t-handle squeegee, and push the head all the way into your chamber from the muzzle. Be sure that the squeegee disk is sideways, or you will deposit all the shell and fill in your barrel directly into your chamber and onto your bolt.

Push gently, and stop immediately when you feel resistance; there is likely a ball in the chamber, and you do not want to crush it. Now, let go of the patch-end, or pull on the handle on the t-handle, and withdraw the squeegee. Slap the squeegee against your leg to fling the goo and shell off, and then wipe it on your pants or jersey to remove the rest of the residue. Repeat as necessary; two times is usually sufficient to remove all the paint. If you have a battle swab, you use it now, only after using the squeegee. When players ram a battle swab into their barrels after a ball break, they push the bulk of the fill and shell fragments back into the chamber, onto the bolt, and into any electronic eyes in the chamber. This is why battle swabs should be used to soak up the last bits of paint for a clean finish, but never used as the first step in cleaning a barrel during a game.

Only insert your squeegee as far as the beginning of the chamber. You can pop the ball in the chamber by slamming into it with the squeegee, creating an even bigger mess than you already had. To gauge how deep is deep enough, without risking the "feel for resistance" method, you can mark barrel depth with electrical tape. Screw one of your barrels into your marker, drop a paintball into the chamber, and then insert the squeegee until you feel the resistance of the squeegee head against the paintball. Be sure that the squeegee head is sideways, as it will be when you use it to clean the barrel, or your measurement will be off by the radius of the disk.

Now take a piece of colored electrical tape and wrap it around the shaft of your squeegee so that the edge of the tape lines up with the crown of your muzzle. Repeat this for any other length of barrel you have, using a different color for each different length. If possible, match the color of tape to the color of the particular barrel.

When you see the edge of the tape line up with the crown of your muzzle, you know immediately to stop pushing and start pulling...preventing smashed paintballs and speeding your cleaning process!

Longer barrels aren't necessarily better. The generally accepted optimum length is between ten and twelve inches, with porting found on virtually all current production barrels. Balls do not have a chance to stabilize as effectively in shorter barrels, and they can destabilize in longer barrels as the force of the compressed air blast drops off. Many two-piece barrels use a second piece, or "tip," that is several thousandths of an inch wider in bore diameter than the largest rear piece.

The effective length of these barrels is essentially only as far as the bore tightly seals around the ball: as long as the rear piece, though the tips perform very necessary functions. The tips provide a controlled environment for the excess gas to vent through the porting. This minimizes the turbulence through which the paintball flies.

Find a barrel length that suits your playing style: short barrels work better than long barrels for snap shooting and playing tightly around your bunker. Two-piece barrels can normally be used without any tips installed, thus shortening them for use on speedball fields.

Barrels longer than 12 inches, such as two-piece barrels with six- to eight-inch front pieces, are very handy on inflatable bunker fields. Press the side of the barrel into the bunker, and watch as the bunker seems to suck the barrel inside of the canvas folds. Lean the barrel into the side of the bunker like this when you shoot at an opponent, and more of the marker (and your goggles) will remain protected by the bunker while you shoot unhindered.

Oil your marker as part of regular cleaning, and when you experience any technical problems. A marker's bolt may fail to lock back between shots when it is not properly lubricated. Most common household oils and firearm oils attack plastic parts such as polyurethane o-rings. The oil you need is specifically designed for paintball markers (available at most pro shops and online) and is labeled as such. Airgun oil is generally safe to use, as those oils are designed to be o-ring and plastic safe as well.

Apply a thin coat of oil to any metal surfaces that rub together, especially springs. Be sure to oil all steel parts to prevent rust—this includes the screws in your grip panels! Wipe off any excess oil, and only oil assembled parts (regulators, etc.) if the instructions call for it; oil harms some regulators and most gauges! Never put oil into your compressed air tank, or on any part of it; oil inside the reservoir will be subject to heat, pressure, and concentrated oxygen—conditions perfect for a dangerous flash fire!

Tighten your marker before every day of play, and watch for bolts and elbows loosening throughout the day. Check all of the bolts on your marker, such as those securing your bottomline, and make sure that none work their way loose. Ensure that your hopper is affixed tightly to your marker. Thumbscrews on hopper elbows help you tighten them during the game, as tools are not allowed on the field.

Make sure the bolts holding your grip frame to the body of the marker are tight as well, as there are parts, such as the sear, in one that must precisely engage parts in the other.

Use tension elbows and feeds, units that feature bolts or collars that tighten around feed necks, to secure your hopper to your marker. Many mid- and high-end markers come with a C-clamp or other device that holds hoppers securely, and many companies offer aftermarket hopper adapters with these features, and some hoppers even use o-rings to help promote a solid connection between hopper and feedneck. Stepping away from a fallen hopper in a tournament can get you eliminated, and at the least, really hurts your ability to play!

Stabilize the input pressure from your air source. Compressed air is less affected by temperature than CO_2, as a change of ten degrees Fahrenheit can affect CO_2 output pressures considerably while not affecting compressed air output pressures at all. The faster you shoot, the faster liquid CO_2 must boil into a gas to exit your CO_2 tank and power the marker. Temperatures can easily change ten, or even twenty degrees in one day in many areas, which affects the output pressures of CO_2 systems, and thus, your velocity. Chronographing frequently keeps your velocities safe and pressures in the ideal range for reliable operation.

Shot to shot differences can be caused from "shoot down," which is the effect (especially on cold days) of your balls flying shorter and shorter distances during rapid shooting. This is partly because CO_2 is endothermic, meaning that it cools off as it changes states from liquid to gas, and the quicker it boils, the cooler it gets—and the less inclined to boil it becomes. It cools the inside of your marker, and doesn't expand as quickly, so your next shot doesn't have quite the same oomph behind it, and the next shot is even slower.

Compressed air doesn't have this problem, but there are things you can do to enhance your marker's performance on CO_2!

To stabilize velocity and operating pressures when using CO_2, look into the purchase of either a remote system or an expansion chamber; both stabilize operating pressures the same way, but through different means. Liquid CO_2 in your regulator and marker adversely affects the consistency of your velocity, and should it suddenly vaporize, the increased pressure may rupture or otherwise harm the affected part.

A remote kit connects your tank to your marker via a pressure-rated plastic, or steel-braided, hose long enough to allow you to carry your tank on your back. Most woodsball harnesses feature CO_2 tank pouches for remote system users, though tank pouches are also sold individually. By carrying the tank pointing up, the liquid is kept on the bottom of the tank far away from the valve. The gas must vaporize to fill the entire inside diameter of the hose between marker and tank, and there is virtually no chance of getting liquid CO_2 into your marker when using a remote.

Expansion chambers are used on CO_2 powered markers in conjunction with bottomline kits. They give the liquid CO_2 additional chambers in which to boil into a gas before reaching critical parts of your marker. By promoting evaporation of the gas before it reaches the marker, you achieve more consistent operating pressures and more stable velocities.

On "low pressure" markers, where a high volume of air at a low operating pressure is used in place of a small volume of air at high pressure, stable input pressure reduces the stress on springs and o-rings in regulators designed to handle the lower pressures. Pressure spikes from CO_2 heating over the course of the day, or from liquid CO_2 flowing into the regulators and then vaporizing, harms many critical parts.

As remotes and expansion chambers accomplish much the same goal, they do not need to be used together.

Look into purchasing a secondary regulator (all tanks have a regulator, so that's the "primary" reg) for regulating pressure with compressed air. The regulator on your tank takes a pressure of 3,000 psi (or greater) and lets out only 200–500 psi (individual cases vary). That is a pressure differential of about 2,500 psi, which is a lot of strain to put on one regulator. With a secondary regulator, any fluctuations in the output of the tank regulator are corrected to provide a more stable and consistent flow into your marker. With an adjustable output tank regulator, adjust the output pressure to between two and three hundred pounds-per-square-inch (psi) more than your marker's input pressure. Use the second reg to regulate this pressure to within the recommended range of input pressures for your marker. By splitting the work between two regulators you improve the efficiency of each, and the overall performance of your marker.

Hot markers are a problem, and sometimes require switching or trimming springs to reduce the velocity to usable speeds. On markers with secondary regulators or adjustable output regulators on the tank, you can reduce the velocity by adjusting the output pressure on these regulators.

If you have adjusted the velocity down as low as your marker will allow you to adjust it and cannot lower it sufficiently by adjusting or installing regulators, swap the velocity spring for a less powerful one. Fieldstrip the marker and locate a long, narrow spring. In stacked-tube markers, the spring is in the lower tube, and its function is to slam the hammer into the valve to open it long enough for a measured volume of pressurized gas to flow through the bolt and propel the ball. If the spring makes the hammer hit the valve too hard, too much gas escapes and the paintball travels too fast.

Switch this spring with a weaker one (or a stronger spring to improve too-low velocities) to solve the problem. Alternatively, you can use metal clippers to snip coils off of the springs, one coil at a time, until the velocity in the "slowest possible" (least tension on the spring) position is 265 fps. Then adjust the velocity up near the field limit.

Hearing air leak down your barrel is disheartening, but can usually be fixed. Check the velocity of your marker, and if you have output/input gauges on your regulators or chambers, check to see if your marker is over-pressurized. Turn down hot velocities and too-high pressures and see if the leak goes away.

If the leak is still there, you may have a damaged or dirty cup seal. To change it, remove the air and paint from the marker, and let the bolt into its resting position. Remove the low pressure adapter or vertical bottle adapter, whatever is in the front of the lower tube of a stacked tube marker. For pumps and other markers, remove the valve assembly from the marker as per the instruction manual's guidelines. Next, remove the valve spring and pin guide (a star shaped piece of metal), followed by the cup seal and the valve pin it is screwed onto. Unscrew the cup seal and replace it with a new one, placing the pieces back into the valve in reverse order from how you removed them. Have an air tech perform this maintenance if you do not feel comfortable with it.

If the bolt does not stay back after each shot, you have one of several problems. Your air source may have too little pressure to operate your marker, so check this first by looking at the HPA gauge, unscrewing the CO_2 tank and feeling its weight, or changing out the 12gram with a fresh one. Fill any tank that is low on air, and check to see if the problem persists. If low tank pressure is not the problem, you may have the velocity set too low, which results in having too little pressure to push the bolt back far enough to be engaged by the sear. Adjust the velocity, within field velocity limits, until the pressure is great enough to effectively operate the marker. You may have too low of an input pressure from your regulator, so test this pressure as well.

The lips on the sear and hammer can wear and round out over the years, resulting in poor reliability for locking the hammer back on the sear. Disassemble the marker and inspect the interface to see if there is significant rounding of lips and shoulders that would preclude a solid lockup. You can replace worn parts, or attempt to sharpen the edges with a fine metal file. The edges should be perfect ninety degree shoulders to function properly.

On Autocockers, check that the backblock is pushed rearward far enough for the lip on the hammer to clear the sear. You can increase the pressure on the ram to push the backblock farther rearward, or you can remove the bolt and unscrew the backblock two turns at a time on the operating rod.

Bolt stick is fixable. Grab the bolt handle and pull it back as hard as you can. Most of these jams are caused when the bolt pinches broken shell pieces or dirt between itself and the chamber.

Pulling the bolt back, then cleaning the chamber, is the safest bet to keep the problem from getting worse. If you cannot manhandle it into position, place the bolt handle against the corner of a bunker or the clean-cut end of a log. Push the marker forward gently, increasing the force until the bolt is free.

Fieldstrip it at this point, being very careful—the mainspring is compressed, and the guts are going to try flying out the back of your marker! Use a battle swab to clean the chamber. Wipe the bolt on a clean cloth, or a clean part of your shirt. Reassemble the marker and keep playing!

Tank o-rings are critical parts that are damaged easily. When you unscrew your tank, often there is a bit of air that rushes out of the ASA and over the tank regulator. In the case of CO_2, this can cause temperature-related damage to the o-ring. Many ASA units have burs on the threads that don't hinder their function, but tear up o-rings. Have plenty of extra o-rings in your toolbox!

Tanks have slightly different dimensions on their regulators, and not all ASA units are built alike, so you may encounter a tank-to-ASA match that leaks even with a fresh o-ring installed on the reg. To overcome this, place a new o-ring loose in the ASA before screwing the tank in place. Between this new seal around the face of the regulator and the ASA, and the normal sealing function of the tank o-ring, your leak will stop.

The air fittings connecting the ASA to the marker input, expansion chambers, regulators, etc, are standard 1/8 inch threaded pipe fittings. If you require a custom setup for air lines to power a paintball cannon and a marker simultaneously, two markers, one marker from multiple air sources, etc, you can use 1/8 inch pipe fittings from pro shops or from the hardware store. Be sure to get pressure-rated pipe fittings meant for handling high pressure compressed gases.

Modifying your marker is a fun way to add a custom look and feel, but be aware that some modifications will render your marker unusable, or field-illegal. Take great care when performing your own milling, air line work, etc, and check with a certified airsmith before removing any metal. If you modify your grip or install an expansion chamber, bear in mind that tournament rules and most field regulations require that you have a trigger guard fully enclosing the trigger. Know what you can do before you commit your marker, your money, and your time, to extreme modifications.

Need extra range? There is only one type of device that adds range to your shots, and that is the kind that imparts back spin to the paintball. Tippmann makes Flatline units, BT Paintball makes the "Apex System," and Galactic Systemz made a Z-Body for Automag markers. When you impart spin to a paintball, you change its kinetic energy, affecting range and flight path.

A longer barrel will not give you better range, nor will regulators, nor a special bolt, and the fallacy that closed-bolt markers shoot farther is pure hype. These may yield better accuracy or more consistent performance, but not greater distance.

Two identical paintballs shot with identical spin (or lack thereof) at identical velocities will travel identical distances regardless of your marker or setup. This is because the paintballs are subject to identical properties of physics: drag and gravity. Nothing in your marker, save a spin imparting device, can affect these immutable laws of science to make one go farther, so ignore advertising that uses fuzzy physics to lure your money away from you!

Shooting around corners is a fun trick, if you can master the curved flight path of a ball affected by a spin-imparting device. Paintballs curve in the direction of their spin—Flatline barrels impart a backspin, which makes balls rise. If you shoot one at an angle, the backspin becomes side spin—the phenomenon employed by the Apex system. Canting the marker to the left imparts a counterclockwise spin. The result is a ball that hooks to the left.

By varying the degree you cant the marker, you vary the curve of the flight path of the ball. Play around with this special property of physics, and you can start to curve paintballs around the edges of distant bunkers with intimidating effectiveness!

HOPPERS

If your electric hopper randomly shuts off or performs inconsistently, you may have a poor connection between your batteries and their terminals. Remove the battery cover and inspect the batteries and their terminals for corrosion, and clean with baking soda and water as necessary. Clean the feed neck to remove any grime over the sensor eye and laser, or clean under the tab that senses paint movement. Ensure that your batteries are fresh (voltage testers are handy for this), and test the hopper. Shake your hopper lightly and listen for the batteries to rattle around, a sure sign that they fit too loosely in their compartment.

When using 9-volt batteries, you can eliminate slop by taking a piece of thin cardboard and making a shim. If you have only a small amount of space to fill, try the cardboard from a cereal box, perhaps folded over two or three times. Stand the battery, or batteries, up on the cardboard and trace the dimensions of their bottoms. If one thickness of cardboard is sufficient, cut out this shape; otherwise, make the shape two or three times longer than the combined thickness of the batteries and then fold it to size. Place this shim under the batteries in the compartment, and test the hopper again.

Take your hopper apart and clean it every time a ball breaks in the hopper or fill gets sprayed up the feed neck. Place the hopper on your white workbench towel, remove the batteries, find a screwdriver that fits the screws perfectly, and back out the screws that hold the two halves of the shell together. Take note of the orientation of circuit boards and the placement of wires, and be careful not to drip any paint or cleaning fluids onto the circuitry. Wipe the plastic shells with a moist paper towel, but do not use Windex or any other cleaning compound unless the compound is specifically designed to clean plastic parts; cleaning agents that are designed for glass or metal can eat away at the plastic and weaken the shell so that direct hits might break through!

Wipe off any residual moisture with a clean cloth, and use a Q-Tip® to clean any dirt or debris from the circuit board or electrical parts. You can use a dental pick or small nail to remove dirt, shell fragments, and other debris from cracks. Keep all cleaning compounds away from the motor. Replace the shells carefully, and function check before using or storing the hopper.

When your hopper elbow spins around on the feed neck, wrap a hose clamp around the elbow over the feed neck and tighten it. Use electrical tape to tape the tab down so it does not snag on clothing or cut you. You may also use a constricting elbow, which uses a bolt to tighten the unit around your feed neck.

If these do not work, remove the elbow and thoroughly clean the feed neck. Now you can use a single strip of one-inch-wide duct tape, wrapped once around the feed neck, to make it larger and increase friction. Install the elbow and hopper and see if it still spins. If so, remove the elbow and duct tape, and clean the feed neck thoroughly; it's time for a more serious solution.

Cut a one-inch-wide strip of sixty-grit sandpaper long enough to wrap around the feed neck once. Apply superglue to the back of the sandpaper and wrap it around the feed neck, sandy side facing out. Let this dry for a few minutes, then put the elbow on over the sandpaper, and your hopper should never spin in place again.

Be sure to trim any excess tape or sandpaper, as excess material may be pushed in the way of the feed neck and impair the feeding of balls.

GOGGLES

Find the perfect-fitting goggle system for your head. Everyone has a differently shaped head, so not all goggle systems feel the same. Go to your pro shop or field and try on as many different goggle systems as you can find. Look for a tight seal against your face, which you can check by putting the goggles on and looking at the seal made around your eyes; you should not be able to see any light between the sealing foam and your skin. Any space here can let shell or fill squirt into your eyes, causing severe injury.

The goggles should also feel comfortable, and be devoid of places that poke or rub unnecessarily when you move your head and talk. Systems with chinstraps are becoming the norm, and all you'll need to finish them off is to add a top strap. Check the profile that the goggles give you by looking at yourself in a mirror while wearing them. Lenses that curve far out in front unduly enlarge your side profile, and unnecessarily wide systems increase your front profile.

Some companies advertise "fields of vision" in the 200 degree range; but think about it, can you actually see behind yourself?

They measure the field of vision from a point farther forward than your eyes will be, unless they bug out of your head. Any number above 180 degrees won't necessarily help, but might—depending on the design of the goggles—stick out unnecessarily far.

The rub here is that these systems are often the only practical choice for players who wear glasses. While a lot of players with corrective lenses just use contacts for the day, those who insist on glasses frequently benefit from these extreme lenses; they give you enough room for your optics! So be sure to wear your glasses when you go to try on new goggles. If the goggles they hand you at the field, or that you try on at the pro shop, don't fit, be sure to ask for a different type of goggle system—your eyes are worth it!

Many goggle systems use soft plastic for the mouth/throat guard areas. These are safe, though you will feel a slight thump on your skin if you get hit there squarely from close range. They are designed this way to promote bounces instead of breaks, and they largely do an effective job. Just don't roll the flexible part up when you play. Though some players will claim that it helps you speak more clearly on the field (can't you just e-nun-ci-ate more?), it will expose your lips, teeth, and throat to direct hits—that's just unsafe!

Never roll the soft plastic up for storage, either, as this can warp it and reduce its protection value. It is designed for a certain degree of flexibility—but not too much. Warping it adversely changes the way it performs when hit.

Fogging is the phenomenon of water condensing on the inside of your lens—the side closest to your eyes. It is caused when hot, moist air from your breath and face (humid air rises, as from your breath) is trapped between your eyes and the lens. When the lens is cool enough (which doesn't even need to be what you might consider "cool"), that humidity condenses on it and creates a dastardly fog. You can't wipe it from the outside, and it's patently unsafe to take your goggles off during the game or even stick your fingers up in there. But there are measures you can take to prevent fog, and to treat it when it happens anyway.

How do thermal goggles work? There are two styles: double-pane lenses, and treated lenses. Both employ vents atop and below the lens to circulate fresh air around your face, moving the humid air out before it has a chance to cool and condense on the lens, and neither has been proven safer than the other.

JT-style double-pane lenses have a thin lens inside of the primary lens, offset from the first (and attached to it) with a ring of foam. The air in between acts as insulation, while keeping some humid air away from the front lens, so that the temperature difference doesn't promote condensation…other factors, like skin oil or dirt on the inside lens (or water getting between the lenses by leaching through the foam) can still cause fogging, though.

The other approach, as employed in the V-Force and similar goggles, is to have a single-pane lens that is coated with a proprietary anti-fog chemical. This chemical is bonded, usually with heat, onto the plastic, and inhibits condensation.

Thermal lenses are great, but still don't completely prevent that haze from forming on the inside of the lens. If your goggles fog in the field, direct your breath straight forward through the vents in the mouth/throat guard in the goggle system.

Keep moving, as the fresh air cycling through your goggles and whisking sweat-moist air away will disperse much of the fog.

Remove any hoods, sock hats, or other headgear that may

obstruct the vents atop the goggles. Trapping the moist air between your eyes and the lens is a large cause of fogging.

Invest in a goggle fan. Plans abound on the internet for making them from computer fans and powering them with nine volt batteries, but the most surefire solution is to purchase one of the several models of specifically designed paintball goggle fans. These circulate moist air out of your goggles, and can be turned on and off with a simple toggle switch.

Scuba divers have long used the spit-trick to keep fog out of their goggles; this is best done on single-pane goggles, lest the spit penetrate the foam layer between lenses in double-pane lenses. Spit onto the inside of the lens, swishing the spit around so that all parts of the lens are covered in a thin film. Wipe it away with a soft towel (not a paper towel). This odd treatment works by leaving an invisible film of spit on the lens, denying fog a place to form.

When cleaning your goggles, never use Windex or other glass cleaners. These chemicals attack the plastic that comprises the lens, as they are chemically formulated to break down just about anything that is not glass. Using Windex and the like will thus ruin the integrity of your lenses, and you will have to buy new ones to avoid the risk of serious injury.

Instead of these chemicals, use plain water or products that are especially designed for paintball goggles. Apply the liquids with fabric towels, as paper towels can scratch the plastic. You should only have to clean the outside of the goggles, and cleaning agents should not contact the inside of the lens. Special defogging sprays for this side of the lens are commonly available; use only those specifically marketed for paintball goggles.

Touching the inside lens leaves skin oils that attract fog, so be careful when working with goggle systems!

Paint fill can stain your goggles and harm your lenses. Clean all goggle surfaces, inside and out, before putting them away for storage. Use only a damp cloth when dealing with double-pane thermal goggles, as water can seep through the foam barrier between the lenses and become trapped where you cannot reach it.

Use a dental pick to remove the o-rings that hold lenses in place. Tools like butter knives and screwdrivers easily slip, gouging and ruining lenses.

Use a goggle bag to protect your lenses from scratches during storage and transport. As not all players have them, you can make an effective goggle carrying apparatus from a t-shirt, and with a bit of creativity you can organize a lot of your soft goods at the same time. Take your neck protector, and pass it between the Velcro flaps on your gloves, so that they slip around on the strap. Then pass your neck guard through your goggles from the top, so that it engages the elastic headband, and similarly attach your other softgoods to the neck guard. Then close it upon its own Velcro flaps, and you have a bundle of softgoods all linked together—no stray pieces to fall out!

Place the softgoods/goggle unit lens-down on a t-shirt, and fold the shirt over it. Tie the sleeves together and tuck the tails in, and you have a protected bundle of goggles and soft goods, and a fresh shirt for the end of the day.

Add your own goggle retention straps to augment the elastic one that holds your goggles on. Some goggles come with chinstraps, but a top strap is also necessary. The elastic strap that comes on goggles holds them on your head, but does precious little to prevent snagged or bumped goggles from rising or lowering over your face. This presents a hazard to your eyes, especially when running through the woods (even more so at night!) that can easily be avoided with the installation of a chinstrap and top strap. A simple fix using Velcro straps is outlined here, but you can use leather straps from tanker helmets, strips of cloth, or most other suitable materials.

Go to your hardware or craft store, and purchase Velcro tie straps. These usually come in a package of six inch lengths in various colors, and feature a hole punched in one end to accommodate the passing through and looping of the other end. Put your goggles on, and feed one of these straps through the bottom-most vent hole that it fits on the left side of your goggles, making sure it is rearwards far enough to be aligned under your chin. Put the end of the strap through the loop, and pull it so that the loop cinches around the goggle frame and you are left with a long strap. Now, do likewise on the corresponding part of the goggle on the right.

The Velcro has two sides: one scratchy, and one soft. Be sure to put the soft side against your skin, the scratchy side facing away. If you end up with scratchy Velcro on your skin, wrap electrical tape around the portion that is not needed to engage the other strap.

Perform this upgrade on the top of your goggles to make a top strap. The chinstrap will prevent the goggles from lifting if a branch snags them. The top strap prevents the goggles from being pushed down, over your nose, when you slide.

Chinstraps keep goggles from flipping off of your head

Go ahead and make your goggles flashy with stainless steel spikes, studs, or other decoration if you like. Most players pass on this, but if you insist on customizing your goggles, avoid anything that dangles. Things like split rings, ghillie material, and leather straps can snag on branches and cause your goggles to dislodge. Other things like rubber pig noses or big rubber ears might not be allowed in tournaments because they could potentially decelerate a paintball and induce a bounce instead of a break. Never modify the lenses in your goggles, cut holes in your goggles, or remove any part of your goggles, and many modeling glues will eat away at the rubber and weaken them…so you might just want to show your flair some other way after all.

Use foam, such as pipe insulation foam, to help your goggles fit your head better. Should one side of your goggles push painfully against your head, consider a new goggle system. If that is not an option, you can pad the sharp edge by super-gluing a bit of insulation foam, car seat foam, or other soft material to the spot. After installing it, put the goggles on and look all around the seal that is made around your eyes by the goggle's foam. If any white space appears between the goggles and your face, throw the system away and get a new one…do not risk an eye injury!

AIR SOURCE

Protect your tank, regulator, and marker with a fill nipple cover. These simple devices range from fancy $10 stainless steel units that lock in place with ball bearings and dangle on chords when not installed, down to the $0.02 rubber bolt covers you pick up at hardware stores. The purpose of a fill nipple cover is to keep water, mud, dust, dirt, and other gunk out of the fill nipple on your HPA tank. When you fill your tank, thousands of cubic inches worth of gas rush into the tank, whisking with it any matter in its way. Dirt that gets blown into your tank can then get propelled into your regulator, damaging o-rings and blocking the proper seal of tight-fitted parts.

The plunger in the fill nipple, that seals the nipple when the tank is filled, is sealed with an o-ring, like many other seals in your regulator and marker. Debris blasted into the tank nicks this o-ring, which causes leaks, and chunks of debris lodged between the plunger and nipple can create air leaks that drain the tank. Covering the nipple with a rubber bolt-protector, like the ones that come with steel cabinet kits or can be purchased for a few cents each at any hardware store, is imperative to prevent serious hassle and expensive damage. Or, feel free to buy the expensive, custom-anodized ones ...

Do you know your marker's operating pressure? Different models and brands require different input pressures to effectively function, and some can be seriously damaged if you screw a standard high-pressure-output tank into them without first regulating the pressure down to their operating range. Read the owner's manual to find out what input pressures are safe and yield the best performance, and then read the specifications on your tank to determine the output pressure. If you can adjust the pressure, adjust it so that there is no chance of over-pressurizing the marker. Often these markers will come with a secondary regulator to take whatever output pressure you feed it down to the input needed to protect the marker.

For a few extra dollars when you buy an HPA tank, you can pop for an adjustable output regulator. Secondary regulators offer another way of adjusting the input pressure to prevent damage from over-pressurization.

Your velocity will change if you switch your tank. Switching between HPA and CO_2 usually produces a noticeable effect, as does switching between tanks of different manufacture. This is because individual regulators yield slightly different output pressures, even when they are the same brand and model. The most dramatic differences come from switching between a high pressure output tank and a low pressure output tank. If you switch air types, or tanks, be sure to re-chronograph before playing again, to be sure your marker is not shooting hot…or shooting too slowly to be competitive. A secondary regulator will help reduce effects of switching between tanks, but cannot regulate the pressure up.

Cold weather affects CO_2. CO_2 boils (goes from liquid state to gaseous state) at -57 degrees Celsius, whereas 02 (oxygen) boils at -183 degrees Celsius…quite a difference! Odds are you won't play in -57 degree weather, but the effects of CO_2's higher boiling point than oxygen (consider that as the boiling point of the standard atmospheric gas used in HPA tanks) is apparent when you shoot fast on a cold day. On cold days CO_2 powered markers can "freeze up," a condition wherein liquid CO_2 enters parts of the marker that should only handle gaseous CO_2, or where the temperature of the internals in the marker drops so low that they no longer function properly. This is exacerbated by fast rates of continuous shooting.

As previously discussed, expansion chambers and remotes help to keep liquid in the tank and gas in the marker, but the only certain solution to preventing freeze-up is to switch to HPA. Other ways to overcome freeze-up include shooting more slowly, and carrying the marker muzzle-up so that the liquid CO_2 does not pour into the marker.

Mounting your CO_2 bottle in a vertical position instead of in a bottomline configuration is also an effective way to minimize freeze-up, as gravity pulls the liquid CO_2 to the bottom of the tank and only the gaseous CO_2 can enter the marker. A clever shopper can locate an inline expansion chamber to use with a bottomline setup when they cannot fit a standard expansion chamber onto their marker, but inline expansion chambers are seldom used due to the variety of other options in gas stabilization.

Have you hydrostatically tested your HPA tanks? HPA tanks must be hydro tested at regular intervals: three years for fiber wrapped tanks unless stamped for five-year tests, or every five years for most metal tanks. CO_2 tanks can also be hydro tested, but generally it is more economically sound to purchase a new tank for a few dollars more than the cost of hydrotesting an old one. The test is performed by certified professionals who hydro test compressed air devices from scuba diving tanks to medical oxygen canisters.

The process involves submerging your tank in a liquid bath and then filling the tank beyond capacity with compressed air while monitoring its integrity with special instruments that search for weak spots and other damage too fine for the eye to see…but bad enough to cause a rupture if not detected in time.

Look at the date stamped on your HPA bottle. It might be buried in DOT code, but it is always present. If you are unsure of the stamp, which will often include month as well as year, ask an air tech at your pro shop or field what the date reads. If you are coming due for a test, pay the nominal fee (around $20 to ensure that your $200 HPA tank is not going to blow up on you is quite reasonable) and get it tested. Ask an air tech about the proper way to dispose of damaged tanks.

Purchase a few extra bottomline-type ASA units. A lot of stores have them loose in the bottom of "junk" or "discount" boxes, and seldom want more than a few dollars for each. If you need to take your tanks on an airliner that mandates you install a device to force the valve on your CO_2 or HPA tanks open, just screw one of these on and it will likely conform to their regulation. Airline policies for transporting compressed air cylinders are growing increasingly strict, however, and now many mandate that the regulators be completely removed from the tank.

If you need to drain a tank for travel, long term storage, or any other reason, you can thread one of these extra ASA units onto the tank and bleed the air out in a controlled fashion.

Is your CO_2 tank empty? HPA tanks feature a gauge that reads the pressure remaining in the tank, but determining how much gas is left in a CO_2 tank is much more difficult. One way is to hold your tank, and an empty tank of the same CO_2 capacity, and feel for a difference in weight. You can be sure that a CO_2 tank is effectively empty if you can depress the fill nipple easily with your fingertip. You can judge how much gas remains in your tank by feeling how much heavier it is than the empty tank.

Determining how much CO_2 remains in your tank while on the field is more difficult, but manageable with practice. Hold the tank vertically with the regulator up, put your ear close to the base of the tank, and lightly tap the tank with a ring or a coin. Listen to the *ting*…it will ring clearly if you are low on air, and sound a bit muddy and have a lower pitch if a good amount of liquid CO_2 remains. Practice this method with tanks of known fill (full, empty, half…) so that you get to know the different sounds they make.

Another sign you are low on CO_2 is when your marker "burps." This is when your bolt does not lock back (due to a lack of operating pressure to fully compress the velocity spring) and instead keeps slamming forward against the valve until it eventually comes to rest on its own. You can also watch for your velocity to drop off, as seen when the paintballs fall shorter and shorter.

A quick fix for burping is to manually cock your bolt and try again (and hope you don't chop a ball), while the only cure is to fill your tank again. And while you're at it, de-gas your marker, field strip it, and make sure the inside surfaces are only lightly oiled and totally free of paint goo and other debris—these might be the cause of your bolt not engaging the sear as well as simple lack of operating pressure.

When your tank leaks from around the pin valve, you may have a piece of debris or ice obstructing a seal. Take a piece of wooden dowel rod, or an unsharpened pencil, place the tip on the pin in the pin valve, and give it a tap with your hand. You don't want to use anything metal, as this will scratch, mar, or otherwise damage the valve. This action will force the valve open, and the compressed air escaping will usually blast the obstruction free. Be sure to wear eye protection while doing this!

When unscrewing your tank, either HPA or CO_2, watch the process and insure that you are unscrewing the regulator from the marker, and not the tank from the regulator. Sporadic cases have been recorded, some with tragic results, of players accidentally unscrewing their tanks from the tank regulators. When a tank separates from its regulator in this manner, the gas inside immediately expels itself out of the neck, creating thrust and propelling the tank like a rocket. This is most prone to happen when the regulator is installed improperly by not having the torque necessary to remain screwed in during normal use, and/or not having the appropriate application of a thread locking compound.

Never put compressed air sources near fire, heaters, or in parked cars in the summer. This is especially imperative for CO_2 canisters, as the heat from a fire or car baking in the summer sun increases the pressure of the gas inside of the cylinder. Tanks are equipped with copper burst disks that rupture when the tanks are over pressurized—they burst before the tank does, venting all of the compressed gas. These are inexpensive to fix, but do not always work right and are no substitute for taking care of a tank. A tank exploding from being over pressurized can kill a person or destroy a car, so keep them away from fires and any place that reaches temperatures above 100 degrees.

In the winter, many players warm their CO_2 tanks by putting them under their clothing between games. As your body temperature is around 98 degrees, this is fine. Dipping the tanks in hot water as some players do is not safe. The temperature increase from the hot water can lead to dangerous over-pressurization, and the water can corrode the steel on many tanks.

Putting a neoprene sleeve over CO_2 tanks is a good form of insulation, but results in keeping the tank cold. As you shoot, the liquid boils off, which makes the CO_2 tank colder (CO_2 changes states endothermically). Sleeves hold the cold inside the tank, which lowers the pressure inside the tank and is counterproductive.

Stickers are a good way to dress up a marker or add pizzazz to your hopper, but should be left off of your tanks. Stickers can hide damage, corrosion, stress marks, discoloration, or other signs of danger. The DOT (Department Of Transportation) specifications sticker affixed to your tank at the factory, and hydro testing certifications, should be the only decorations of any kind on your tank. You can protect the tank from scrapes, scratches, bumps and abrasions with neoprene or cloth covers, and decorate those all you want! Many airsmiths will not work on or fill a tank with stickers on it because of the possibility that the stickers could hide signs of danger.

Make a cool, custom tank cover from the sleeve of a camo jacket. If you have an old jacket, or one you want to make sleeveless, cut off a sleeve and slip your tank inside. Measure how much of your sleeve you need to use to fold the end over the base of the bottle and sew it shut, and then make your second cut. Stitch one end together, and then cut a series of ten to twelve small holes around the lip of the open end. Keep these holes from fraying by outlining them with superglue. Pass a black shoelace through these holes, and you now have a drawstring closure to keep the cover on your tank!

Players who are more intrepid with a needle and thread can use part of the front of a BDU jacket, or the thigh part of extra-small camo pants, which can give you a handy pocket on the side of the tank cover. You can store spare o-rings in a film canister in this pocket, or any number of small parts and widgets.

PAINT

Keep your paintballs intact at the field by storing them wisely between games. Prolonged exposure to direct sunlight weakens the shells on paintballs, making them more prone to breaking in your marker. Humidity in the air also undermines their quality, causing balls to swell and soften slightly so they may fit too tightly in your bore or bind up in your feed tube. Humidity also makes paintballs more inclined to stick together, and soft paintballs are more likely to bounce off of your opponents than break on them!

Store paintballs in airtight sealed plastic bags, and store them out of direct sunlight. Beverage coolers work well to store paintballs while at the field: the insulated containers keep the heat of the day from melting the paintballs, or the cold of the winter from freezing them (which makes the shells more brittle when they thaw), as well as keeping the paint out of direct sunlight.

Keep paintballs sealed against humidity

For long term storage, use 4mil-thickness plastic bags, like the bags most paint comes in. This thickness of plastic keeps air from diffusing through the plastic and affecting the paintballs, so long as you close the open end securely with a heat sealer, wire twist ties, etc. Storing paint in tubes is acceptable for short term storage, but even overnight is too long for this form of storage during multi-day tournaments where paint quality counts!

If you store paint in bulk for extended periods of time, be sure to rotate your paintballs every four months. Simply flip bags and cases of paint upside down without otherwise disturbing them so that as the fill settles, it will not settle permanently on the "bottom" of all of your paintballs. If the paint settles, your balls will wobble in flight and your accuracy will suffer greatly.

Never pick paint up off the ground and put it in your marker. Fine dirt and sand stuck to the ball can wreak havoc on your bolt and other internal parts. Oftentimes balls on the ground soak up moisture, causing soft spots that lead to barrel breaks, increased drag feeding into your chamber, and destabilized flight—if by some miracle they make it out of your barrel in the first place. Load carefully, and consider any paint on the ground to be spoiled.

Avoid sticking your hands into the bag of paint when filling pods and hoppers. Oil, sweat, and dew from your hands introduce moisture to paintballs. Cornstarch shells are less finicky when it comes to handling moisture, but the dirt and sand you introduce to the paint is detrimental to proper marker function. Use a pod speed-loading funnel, or pour the paint in the pods very carefully.

When you have a case with four compartments, prop your empty pod in the center of the box, leaning against the cardboard divider in the middle. As you pour the paintballs into the pod, any that spill will be collected in the cardboard box instead of falling onto the wet ground. These can be manually loaded into your pods or hopper.

When loading your pods, load until there is one inch of space between the paintballs and the lid. Close the pod, place it vertically between your hands, and spin it gently. This settles the paint, and helps you fit more balls into the pod. Also, with the paint better settled, each ball is under more evenly distributed pressure and is thus less likely to break in the tube or rattle when you run. When you close the lid, make sure there is very slight pressure on the stack of paintballs: this slight pressure will help keep them from rattling, which makes you a quieter player and decreases the odds that one will break in the pod from bouncing around.

When you buy a case of paint, immediately inspect each bag by picking them up and looking over every ball you can see. There will likely by brown or green spots in places on the inside of the plastic where packing oil pools, but ignore them. You are looking for any broken paintballs, as evidenced by any amount of fill oozing between balls or down the inside of the bag. It is within the bounds of politeness to ask for a replacement bag if you find one containing broken paint. Many field owners inspect each bag as a professional courtesy before selling them to you.

Face the tabs on your pods towards your body in your harness. When you pull open the flap holding your pod in place, you can catch the latch to the lid in the process and dump the entire pod! Avoid this by inserting the tube so the tab faces your body. When you draw the tube, be sure to firmly grasp the collar, not just the leading edge (the lid).

The best paint still gets chopped, dropped, or occasionally breaks in the barrel. Carry a good squeegee in every game, and clean it thoroughly after every use. Use water to get the paint and shell off, then wipe the entire length of the squeegee with paper towel to remove any grease or slime.

CLOTHES

Proper padding is essential to playing safely and having fun. Consider anatomical vulnerabilities, and look into wearing an athletic cup or chest protector. Athletic cups are essential gear for male players, as the consequences of taking a direct shot to the crotch often include embarrassing and painful medical attention. Invest in quality knee and shin guards, elbow pads, neck protectors, and consider the so-called "body armor."

Kneepads allow you to get into difficult positions, dive more safely behind cover, and crawl with comfort. They offer protection to two of the most important joints in your body, and are indispensable for front players and woodsball snipers. Kneepads that also incorporate shin guards are popular among both tournament and woodsball players. The danger of landing with a limb or rock under your shin is great, and these guards are generally rigid enough to prevent broken limbs and a majority of bruises.

Kneepads are always a good idea—be aware that some rule sets make you wear them on the outside

Elbow pads enable you to crawl with comfort and safety, while neck protectors offer shielding for Adams Apples in males and sensitive skin for both genders. Tournament players primarily take hits to their goggles, markers, hands, and necks, making pads and gloves for those body parts vital to playing with safety and comfort.

Body armor is often cumbersome, hot, and awkward. Younger players occasionally wear it while they toughen up to getting hit, and referees at big games have been known to pad-up to avoid the discomfort of multiple hits when they get caught in crossfire. Look for body armor that offers real protection, with good ventilation so you don't overheat in the summertime. Also check the range of motion it offers, so that in normal playing positions (kneeling, crawling, leaning sideways…) it won't rub or bunch up uncomfortably.

For paintball clothes on a budget, check out an Army/ Navy surplus store for used camouflage. Tournament players can find solid-color cargo pants and other articles that look sharp with jerseys, without having to spend the big bucks on paintball-specific clothing. You can also find unique hats and extra thick hiking socks that significantly reduce blisters when you play all day in boots, as well as all manner of gear you can use in scenario games or rec ball.

Choosing clothes that are good for paintball is challenging; jeans just aren't as universal as you think. Ideal pants for paintball are roomy, without extra material that gets in the way. Put on the pants you intend to make part of your outfit, and do the splits as low as you can go; your body should be your limit, not the pants. Now run at least one block in your pants, as fast as you can, and feel for chafing, restriction, and if any extra material gets in the way. Feel the fabric, and ask "will this material withstand sliding around in the forest or over grass and turf on a speedball field?"

Wind pants are less than ideal, as they offer little protection against the stickers in the forest, and shred when you slide over the debris on the forest floor. Cotton pants are cloth armor for the woods and will slide through just about anything and come out just fine, but they hold moisture like sponges. Many companies make synthetic speedball pants specifically cut and designed for paintball. Virtually all paintball pants have double stitching, reinforcement on the knees, and loops for belts.

When looking for a paintball shirt, consider the jersey vs. camouflage debate, and then settle on a top that is well made and suits your style of play. Some jerseys integrate thin elbow pads into their material, and cloth BDU tops are great to guard against the stickers and brambles in the forest. In jerseys, look for material that will "breathe" so your sweat does not get trapped against your body. Some jerseys offer vent holes, or are made from materials, similar to hockey jerseys, that offer great ventilation.

Put the jersey on and look for a fit that leaves a minimum of excess material hanging off of you (baggy jerseys catch balls you don't want to catch). The cut should have room enough to slightly billow in the wind, as a skin-tight fit will not promote bounces or feel comfortable (and usually does not look good either!), but not so much as to snag on branches or create excess ruffles that catch paint.

Camouflage tops should adhere to the same rule for balance between loose comfort and close cut to avoid snagging on brambles and limbs as you dash through wooded fields. The pockets on camo tops are good for holding paintgrenades, smoke grenades, o-ring kits and other gear you need on the field, but are not appropriate for holding unprotected paintballs. Dumping loose paintballs into your pocket not only makes the paint dirty, but also leaves a gooey, useless mess in your pocket if you get shot there, lay on the pocket while crawling, etc.

Button the jacket and bend forward slightly. Hook your arms in front of you and flex your muscles like a bodybuilder. If the jacket is too tight, the back will prevent you from bringing your hands together, or you will rip the jacket in half. Either way, it's a sign of a too-tight-fit. Go one size larger.

Snow-slicked surfaces and indoor fields that use artificial floor materials present unique traction problems for running quickly and cornering well. Combat boots are great for summer use, but many styles lack the proper traction for snow, ice, and slick mud. Look into shoes and boots that are designed for indoor soccer when you play on artificial turf, and track shoes for well maintained speedball fields. Consider special snow boots for winter.

Clean hits off of your clothes between games by wiping the paint with your fingers. If this does not satisfactorily remove the mark, such as when you get a white break on a black shirt, rub some dirt onto the spot to soak up more paint and add a little dark stain so that referees will be less likely to call you eliminated for the old hit.

Creatively clean hits from your clothing and gear, and stay cool in the summer time too! Go to a hardware store and purchase a hand-pump poison sprayer for pest control use, but only buy a new one that has never had poison put through it! The plastic body will hold a respectable amount of water, and after pumping it by hand, you will be able to spray a fine mist of clean water out of a long nozzle. Use this sprayer to wash paint from small areas of your clothes between games, or spray on your teammates to keep them cool on hot days. Be sure to decorate the sprayer with lots of paintball stickers and a large sign that says "for water use only, never add poison" to prevent it from ever getting contaminated!

Before any game, especially for tourneys, have a teammate inspect your outfit for hard spots. Big belt buckles, the plastic buckle fasteners on some harnesses, metal studded belts, etc, are all ideal places for paintballs to break. Cross-field lob shots often bounce off your stomach, thighs, and other soft places, but if those same balls hit a buckle or hard spot, they will break. Remove anything that can catch or break a ball that might otherwise bounce!

Paintball jerseys are great, but for team apparel on a budget, look outside of the paintball industry. A fresh team can still look attractive with customized, uniform t-shirts...and often, you can get your team logo and players' names on a t-shirt far cheaper than on an expensive paintball jersey.

Look in the yellow pages for a local t-shirt printer or monogram shop. Quality customized jerseys are also offered by independent printers, and often these jerseys both look cool and offer the kind of performance that you need for paintball. You can customize these blank jerseys as much as your wallets can handle to make catchy uniforms you can guarantee no one else wears.

For play during cold winters, you'll need to layer-up your clothing. Avoid the classic cotton "long johns" thermal underwear at all costs—the material binds between your legs, holds sweat against your body, and is uncomfortable for running. Go to a sporting goods store and purchase the thermal underwear marketed for joggers and trekkers, and look specifically for any that claim to "wick" water away from your skin. These types of material actually move sweat away from your skin, which reduces the chaffing and rashes you get from playing all day with wet under-things stuck against your body. They are also made of material that stretches more readily than cotton, which lets you run just as fast as you do in the summer!

Stay in the game after a ball "bounces" off of you. While local rules may differ, the universal bounce rule is that if a ball bounces off of your gear or body without breaking, you are still in the game. Cold weather games see a lot of bounces, as players layer up with padded coats and thick sweatshirts. Wearing a pair of sweatpants under your regular paintball pants can promote bounces off of your legs, and thick coats promote bounces off of your upper body. It's not cheating as long as you are actually dressing for the weather, though most tournaments (even in the winter) have a rule limiting the amount of clothing you can wear.

Headgear protects your head, keeps you warm, and promotes bounces! The bill on a baseball cap, when worn backwards with a goggle system in place, helps to protect the back of your neck. A sock hat, beanie, or other soft headgear protects from the thump of hits, prevents sunburn for folks with short hair, promotes bounces, and keeps you warm in cool weather. Wear something on your head for protection and bounces, and give yourself a bit of style in the process.

Be sure that the headgear does not interfere with the vents on your goggles, or the lens will fog. Avoid putting your goggle strap over hats, as branches can snag on your hat and rip it, and your goggles, right off of your head. Be sure that your choice in headgear does not interfere with the security or function of your goggle system!

OTHER

Store loose Allen keys, small o-ring sets, and tiny tools in a spare pod. Label the pod accordingly, and you have a compact, secure travel case for the odds and ends that rattle around in the bottom of your toolkit!

Use colored zip ties to indicate the status of tanks. A yellow zip tie fastened around the neck of an HPA tank, when placed there by an airsmith after date and condition inspection, can indicate that the tank is a 3,000 psi unit, while a green zip tie can indicate that the tank is a 4,500 psi unit. The presence of the zip tie indicates that an airsmith has inspected the tank's hydro dates and condition, while the color codes for a safe fill pressure. This saves significant amounts of time later in the day when lines grow long. With effective removal of all existing zip ties, and installation of your specific ties, you can eliminate the need to repeatedly remove cumbersome tank covers.

Clip off all colored zip ties, paper or plastic bands, and other labels after you are done playing in a given event. This saves confusion at chrono and air fill stations later when referees have to wonder what a yellow zip tie means around your regulator, or why there is a green plastic band passed through your trigger guard.

When you only have one color of zip tie for indicating the fill pressure of HPA tanks, only put it around the neck of 4,500 psi tanks (if your field can fill to that pressure). If a referee fails to put a zip tie on a 4,500 psi tank, it will then be filled to only 3,000 psi...a safe pressure. Should you mark the lower pressure tanks only, then the "no zip tie default" is 4,500 psi, a very dangerous pressure for 3,000 psi tanks.

Colored zip ties can also be used to code markers for chrono checks, as the presence of a zip tie around the trigger guard may indicate that the person chronoed onto the field at a safe speed. A different color can be used to indicate nighttime speed restriction compliance, or other special conditions. Keep the system simple, and make sure all the refs understand what the colors mean, and this tip can greatly simplify fills and chrono procedures while increasing safety.

Inspect the nets every morning, and use zip-ties to fix holes

When filling tanks that are color-banded to show they've been inspected, and color-coded to show pressure, wrap a few of the same-color zip ties around the appropriate air station hoses. That helps eliminate confusion: green-banded tanks are only filled by green-banded hoses, and only by the field's trained refs or airsmiths.

Store batteries so that their contacts do not touch each other, or any other electrically conductive material. Batteries carried loose in a pocket with change, or in a tool kit with metal tools, have a nasty habit of forming short circuits that rapidly drain them and often produce intense heat.

Protect batteries by storing them in a fishing tackle box, or a plastic storage unit specifically designed to store batteries. Keeping them in their original packaging until ready for use also works, and helps you keep track of fresh batteries from not-so-fresh similar batteries.

Use empty paintball cases for storage around the house and when you move—just be sure to label them appropriately! The uniformity of the boxes and the strength of their construction make storage simple while protecting your property.

Use empty cases as trash receptacles—at the end of the day, throw away the box, trash and all.

Silencers are neat, but dangerous from a legal standpoint. Firearm silencers are tightly restricted, and lawful owners of these silencers must register them with the government and pay hundreds of dollars in special taxes. Paintball silencers are technically governed by such laws, though are easily made by or purchased from creative players. Be aware that federal law defines a silencer as any device capable of "noticeably" suppressing a firearm's report.

If a firearm can be shot through your paintball silencer with the effect of reducing the report, you are violating a federal law and can be jailed for ten years, fined $100,000, or both. Many players still use silencers for scenario games and backyard shooting, but depending on the pugnacity of local prosecutors, they could face a lot of trouble.

To lower the noise created by your marker without using a silencer, invest in a quality ported barrel. Keep the internal parts of your marker clean and lightly oiled. Some low pressure operating system conversions reduce the operating noise of markers as well.

Before investing in smoke grenades, paintgrenades, or paintmines, check with your local field or the organizers of the event you plan to travel to and ensure that such devices are allowed for play at their fields.

Transport paintmines, paintgrenades, and the like, in the trunk of your car, in an old paint case or labeled appropriately in a regular box. If you are stopped by police and they search your car, tell them what they'll find, and stress that it's just paintball equipment—you don't want them stumbling across paintmines and/or "military simulation" (mil-sim) gear and assuming the worst!

If you intend to use a smoke grenade, check the field conditions. Most smoke grenades use fire to create the smoke, which presents a hazard on fields with dry brush, dry grass, or other flammable material. Field owners are also hesitant to allow incendiary devices near inflatable bunkers! If the conditions present a fire hazard, eschew smoke grenades in favor of paintgrenades.

Be especially careful when using a smoke grenade while wearing a ghillie suit, or any time when playing against someone with a ghillie suit. These suits are notorious for catching fire easily; fire prevention and other ghillie-specific tips can be found in the Woodsball section!

Paintgrenades can be rigged as mines with the right know-how. There are two types: those where a rubber band secures a coil of body-tube, so that when impact energy dislodges the rubber band, the coil comes undone and sprays paint from the end,

501 PAINTBALL TIPS, TRICKS, AND TACTICS

and the type where a BB is used to plug the end of the tube, so that the impact energy dislodges it to release the paint. The rubber band styles include the Atomic Ordnance® grenades, while the ball bearing ones include the Tippmann Squadbuster® and similar models. Those with rubber band closures are ideally suited for booby traps, though both styles can be used in setups where the grenade is dropped as part of the trap.

Place a paintgrenade, top pointing toward where your target will be, in a bunker, building, or the side of a trail. Tape it to a tent stake or short, pointed stick, then use that to anchor the grenade to the ground. You can also tape them, or use rope to tie them, to sticks in stick bunkers, door frames, etc. Tie a piece of fishing line around the rubber band. Tie the other end of the line to a log, large stick, tree trunk, or other relatively immobile object. If the force required to remove the rubber band from the grenade is less than the force required to move this anchor object, your setup will discharge properly.

For paintgrenades that have ball bearings plugging the ends, remove their safety cap or clip and massage the ball bearings to get paint around them, making them slicker and easier to dislodge. Put it in the crooks of tree branches, over door frames, on window ledges, etc, where the tripwire will make it fall, the impact energy dislodging the BB and setting it off. When your opponent catches his foot on the trip wire, it will drop down right next to him and squirt his legs. Use variations on this theme to booby trap castle entrances, props, and other things on the field.

More tips on setting traps can be found in the Woodsball section!

Mark your barrels, pods, squeegees, tanks, Allen keys…any gear that can be confused with another player's stuff, or "walk" away when you turn your back. An effective way to mark your gear is with coded bands of colored electrical tape. You can also add a nice custom, patriotic, or celebratory touch to your stuff while marking it as yours.

Buy your favorite colors in electrical tape, or purchase the colors in the scheme of the United States flag, or the flag of whatever country your ancestors are from. The key to marking your gear personally is that it will stick out from everyone else's, so be creative and obscure. Standardize a sequence of colors, such as the author's use of black, red, and yellow, top down, to celebrate his German ancestry. Wrap your first color around the collar of your pod, the rear (before the first porting holes) of your barrels, around the shaft of your squeegee…then wrap the second color below that, etc, for all colors in your code. Two colors are sufficient, but three or four colors in a code will identify your gear if other teammates mark their stuff in similar fashions.

You can also mark your pods with identical bumper stickers. Stickers are not effective for marking squeegees, barrels, or tanks. Electrical tape can be unwrapped from gear for damage inspections; stickers cannot, and especially should not be used on tanks.

The lids on many pods are affixed to collars that slip onto the end of the tube. If you use this sort of tube, be aware that over time the collar will work a bit loose from the tube and may wear to the point of slipping off the pod when you pull it from your pack. Dumping a hundred and forty balls in the middle of the game is embarrassing and expensive, but is easily avoidable. Use three to four drops of super glue or plastic epoxy to secure the collar to the body of the tube.

Stock players reload their markers with ten round tubes, usually under fire, and seldom with the advantage of looking at what they are doing. Picking up these tubes and their small, green caps after games is a time consuming, tedious task. Stockers in scenario and big games have to jam the caps and tubes into their pants or else lose them forever. The caps, which blend into the grass, are crucial to using the tubes and are easily lost. Rectify this with a simple rubber band fix. Acquire a rubber band with a two inch or larger diameter, one ten round tube, a roll of electrical tape, and super glue.

Drip the glue on one quarter inch of the rubber band, and affix it to the body of the tube at least one inch down from the mouth. Repeat this on the opposite end of the rubber band, affixing it to the top of the cap. Allow it to dry for one minute, then wrap a single layer of black electrical tape around the tube, covering the place you secured the rubber band. This prevents the rubber band from coming off of the tube during rough handling.

The inch of space between the mouth of the tube and where the rubber band is affixed is crucial, as this space is inserted into the feed tube of the marker to open the loader gate. If you arrange the rubber band so that it holds the cap on under pressure, you can use sandpaper to slightly narrow the mouth of the tube and to enlarge the inside of the cap. This will make the cap fit more loosely, and come off more easily; the rubber band then functions as well to hold the cap on when the tube is loaded. Store these tubes with the caps dangling free so as to not wear out the rubber bands or stress the glue joints.

Go clean your squeegees. If you have time to read this chapter, you have time to clean your squeegees and swabs, and are likely comfortable and not rushed at the moment; these conditions are hard to match at the field! Wipe the shafts of your squeegees, and thoroughly clean their rubber disks. If you have cloth patches on your squeegees, rinse them several times, wringing them out between rinses, and allow them to dry completely. Rinse your battle swabs in the sink with a drop of laundry detergent, wringing all the paint, dirt, and oil out of the fibers. Allow these to dry as well. A dirty swab or squeegee will make a bigger mess than you had before!

Flexible-center-type battle swabs frequently suffer from separation issues where one of the swabs pulls out of the flexible hose that connects them. Rectify that by squeezing three drops of super glue into the hose and quickly jamming the swab back in place. Do this for both swabs on these units.

You can make a pod-swab from a cloth towel and a piece of PVC pipe. Purchase an inexpensive thick-pile hand towel and a one-foot section of 1 inch diameter PVC pipe. Use super glue to securely attach the towel to the PVC pipe, wrapping the towel several times if needed, to ensure a tight fit in your pods. To clean a pod, insert the unit and spin it around to soak up broken paint or water.

Your harness can carry water bottles as well as tubes and paintgrenades. Just swap a 12oz. bottle of water for a pod, and you can take a drink with you around the staging area for last-minute hydration, or use your harness to carry water bottles to teammates or referees at big games.

When you find a water cooler, but no cups, use a small amount of water to rinse the inside of an empty pod and drink from it; they make great emergency cups. Be sure to dry the pod before filling it with paint again.

Bring newspapers or a drop cloth to sit on in your car to keep the mud off of your seats.

TACTICS

SHOOTING

Have a solid stance any time that you are in position behind a bunker. Twisting to dodge paintballs and sliding around to make shots is critical when players shift and advance on you. Maintaining balance through a solid position is essential to moving quickly without falling over.

Avoid kneeling on both knees at the same time, and sitting on your butt. You cannot move quickly from these positions, and will be a sitting duck if you get bunkered or an opponent makes a bold move to get an angle on you. Keep at least one foot flat on the ground as often as possible so you can lean, dive, and sprint on an instant's notice.

Instinct shooting. Few paintball markers have sights of any kind, so players rely on instinct shooting, or the ability to shoot accurately by feel and familiarity. The only way to get good at instinct shooting is to practice, starting with a focus on the fundamentals. Go to the target range, with your goggles and lots of paint, and square up to a target.

Take a small step forward with your left foot, leaving your right foot planted. Flex your knees, and find a comfortable stance. Now raise your marker and put the tank against your shoulder, all the while staring at your target. Keep both eyes open and bring your marker to bear, looking down the side of the barrel and never taking your eyes off of the target.

Squeeze off a single shot, and watch where it hits. Adjust your marker and shoot another ball, repeating the process until you hit the target. Now freeze, and take careful note of your position. If anything feels uncomfortable, change it until you feel natural pointing the marker directly at the target. Shoot three balls, slowly, taking note of all the elements of the position. Lower your marker.

Stare directly at your target during the entire drill. If your target is large, such as a tree or a trashcan lid, find one particular feature of the target to stare at: an existing paint splotch, knot, hole, mark…By limiting your focus to a small area, you tighten the tolerances of your accuracy. Beginners can normally keep their shots within three inches of their target at a practical distance. If the target is a six inch steel plate, they should hit it most of the time. But, if the target is a sticker in the middle of the six inch plate, they should hit the plate every time.

Repeat this exercise until you can hit the target with your first shot every time, and then speed up the drill: snap your marker into place while assuming the shooting posture, and instinctively touch off a shot the instant you feel "on target." When you get the hang of this, add different elements: shoot smaller targets, farther targets, try shooting from the kneeling position, etc. The ultimate goal is to be able to shoot instinctively, accurately, from both your right and left hands. Focus on the fundamentals!

Look down the far side of your marker to aim when snap-shooting. This is counter intuitive, as your natural inclination is to look along the near side, like the left side of your marker when shooting right handed. Look down the right side of your marker, so that your marker is actually in line with your nose. Notice that this automatically cants your marker so that your hopper is behind cover…which provides much less of a target for your opponent.

The hopper is tucked tighter, and the angle on the feed is no more extreme than if you leaned the marker to the right to sight down the left side. With practice, you can train yourself to shoot just as accurately this way.

This also increases your snapshooting accuracy and tactical movement, as you can sneak a peek out the side of your bunker without lowering your marker (which would make you defenseless, and throw off your accuracy when you shoulder it again) or exposing it to what might be a surprise hail of paint. If you see a good time to strike, just lean out a bit farther and your marker is on target. If you dodge back, your marker was not really exposed in the first place, minimizing the target your opponent had to hit…and eliminating the warning (from a hopper popping out) that you were snapping around.

Pick a distant reference when you shoot a lane. Trees, bunkers on other fields, etc, provide good aiming points. When you shoot the lane, aim at that distant target to keep your paint where you need it. Shooting without such a focus leads to your shots drifting left and right down the lane, creating gaps in the stream through which a player can slip without getting tagged.

Use reference points when snapshooting—it really helps! Find a feature of your opponent's bunker, intermediate obstacle, or other object in sight that corresponds to the player's location. Pros find marks on the edge of their bunkers that correspond to the position of an opponent. Before snapping out, line your marker up to aim at this reference point. Now when you snap out, you already have the proper elevation to put a ball on target, and all you need to do is adjust a little bit for windage to hit your opponent!

Walking the trigger is a shooting method where you use the index and middle fingers of your shooting hand to tap the trigger as quickly as you can. Practice this on the target range by placing the pads of your index and middle fingers on the trigger with your other fingers hovering in midair. Support the marker with your non-shooting hand. Press the trigger with your index finger. Now press it with your middle finger. Find a rhythm by drumming your fingers, one at a time, on the trigger as fast as you can manage.

Once you get the feel for this, wrap your other fingers around the grip of your marker. Your speed will slow with the changing ergonomics, but your shooting hand should maintain a strong hold on your marker at all times during a game—it helps you aim, and keeps you from dropping it!

Use two fingers to "walk" the trigger when you need to increase ROF in semi-only mode

Fanning your trigger is another way to increase your rate of fire while locked in semi-automatic mode, but also has the disadvantage of decreased accuracy inherent from not holding the marker securely with your shooting hand. Extend your index, middle, and ring fingers on your shooting hand, and lower your ring finger slightly below your middle finger while slightly raising your index finger. Now your fingers form three steps. Draw your fingers simultaneously rearward against your trigger and downwards toward the trigger guard. Each fingertip will hit in succession, giving you a three shot burst each time you "fan" the trigger with your fingers.

When first-shot accuracy counts, shoot with only your index finger and wrap the rest of your fingers comfortably around the grip. Walking the trigger is great to impress friends at the range, but few players can walk the trigger with the kind of accuracy needed for one-shot-hits during intense snapshooting showdowns. The traditional one-finger-shooting grip helps you point the marker faster, hold it steadier, and make the minute adjustments critical to improving accuracy. Save the fanning and walking for laying cover fire and suppressing lanes.

Practice tight snapshooting with a mirror and your couch. Most people would rather play than run drills all Saturday, so run this drill at home during the week. Set a large mirror opposite your couch, then completely unload your marker, put your goggles on (you need to practice how you will play), and assume a tactical position playing the couch as a bunker. Snap around and "engage" your reflection in the mirror.

Hold and study your position, paying attention to how much of your body and marker you expose. You are your own opponent; make yourself as small of a target as possible, then practice snapping around and presenting only this tiny target profile. It really helps to have this "opponents' view" of yourself as you practice doing the basics better!

PLAYING

Pick your team well! A team of all front players is going to get rolled time and again, as will a team of all back players. Consider the size of the field and the first bunker positions, looking for strength in forward bunkers (for front players), rear bunkers (for back players), or midfield bunkers (for insert players).

When you pick your team during open play, or throw friends together the morning of a local tourney, pick your team based on having a healthy balance of front/back/insert players, and decide what strengths you need based on the layout of the field. By fielding a balanced squad, you will have the groundwork for an ideal dynamic between movers, shooters, yellers, and crawlers.

Get ready to charge down the field by assuming a sprinter's position at your start station. Start station rules vary, with some formats demanding players look away from the field, face away from the field, have their markers touching the start station, or conform to any of a myriad of other regulations.

In any event, assume a posture like you would if getting ready to run a race. Bend your knees and lean toward your first bunker. Put your weight slightly forward, but don't exaggerate your posture—leaning too precariously will make you stumble on your first step rather than dart away.

Bounce on your toes when the referee begins the countdown. Bouncing loosens your leg muscles, increases your heart rate, and releases a bit of adrenaline, all of which give you an extra push when you hear "go!"

Beware of the "ostrich fallacy," where you are lured into thinking that your opponents can't see you simply because you can't see them. Tuck your arms, especially your elbows, and your ankles behind your bunker! And remember that any bunker may conceal an opponent, so don't lose track of their positions.

Do not double up in bunkers, unless you absolutely must. With two players in the same bunker, an opponent with an angle behind the bunker can get two of you instead of only one. Also, instead of you and a teammate having different angles on opponents, you have essentially the same angles, decreasing your tactical effectiveness to essentially one player.

The positive side to doubling up in a bunker is that one of you can cover each side, providing very effective protection against bunkering maneuvers and using a well-positioned bunker to put pressure on two sides of the field at once. If one of you gets dropped, the other can fill in and work the whole thing. Do not shoot out of the same side of the bunker as your partner, unless he shoots over the top of you while you run or crawl to another bunker.

Keep one player on each side to counter bunkering moves

Good bunkers to double up in, when you have to, are snakes and center flag stations. One player can secure the head of the snake while the other crawls along it. The rear player protects the crawling player from getting bunkered or shot by an opponent elsewhere in the snake. With two players in the flag station, one can play a counter-bunkering role or look for unique cross-field shots on the tapelines while the other player focuses on getting the flag. If one player gets dropped, you have another right there to secure the flag.

Trace the paint back to who is shooting at you. When you only see a stream of paint coming, but cannot afford to stick your head up to see which bunker is shooting at you, watch the flight path of the paintballs and extend that line to get a picture of where you are taking fire from. Snap out with your marker pre-aimed at that spot, and if the stream continues, shoot toward where you think it originates.

Offensive blind shooting is an offensive move when you can see where your balls are going but cannot necessarily see where they end up when they fall behind intermediate bunkers. Unlike regular (defensive) "blind shooting," where a newbie sticks his marker around a bunker and manically fans the trigger, offensive blind shooting is a great way to drop shots over intermediate bunkers and clip opponents…or put them back in so you have a bit more room to maneuver.

Walking shots is an effective way of adjusting your point of aim, but often takes too much time during intense firefights and heated tournaments. To walk your shots onto a target when the pace is a bit slower, shoot a steady stream of paint and take note of where it hits. Adjust your point of hold, while continuing to shoot, and watch your stream of paint "walk" toward your opponent.

There is usually no time to walk your shots onto your target. Once you shoot a volley, snap back immediately after the last shot and let your paint do what it will. Your natural tendency is to stay exposed and watch the paint hit to confirm an elimination, but this exposes you to other opponents and any paint your foe already has in the air. Snap out, shoot, and snap back while your paint is still in the air. Good back players will let you know when you get your opponent.

Start sprints correctly by ensuring proper balance and form when you burst out of your bunker. When you start a sprint from the kneeling position, the first step you take is the most critical. Pay attention to which leg is going to take the first step in your run. You use one leg to stand while taking your first big step with the other leg. The stepping leg should be on the "front field" side of your body, while the supporting leg should be on the "back field" side. Try this: snapshoot right handed around your right side of a bunker. Before you sprint downfield and toward the right tapeline, crouch so that your left knee is on the ground and your right foot is planted. Lunge!

Notice that you have good speed and balance. Now try the same thing with your left leg planted and your right foot taking the first step. As your body tries to twist to go downfield instead of directly toward the tapeline, the natural inclination is for your right foot to try swing into your left leg and make you fall.

Remember, the leg that is closer to your start station should form a solid brace for you to lunge with while the leg closer to your bunker should be the first leg you step with—never trip out of your bunker again!

No buddy? Give yourself cover fire! Shoot at the guy who has you pinned. He will duck. Now move, keeping your marker up and shooting. You can usually make your next bunker since he is ducking and not shooting, so keep the heat on him for extra protection. This move is called "powering in."

Leapfrog! Advance down the field in teams of at least two. The player in front should shoot to suppress any opponents who are in range while the player behind advances as far as possible.

This player, when able, should shoot to suppress any threatening opponents while the now-in-back player advances past him. Repeat until you reach the other team's flag station!

Regain control when someone is posted on you, or else your head will be down while the other team gains massive ground. Pro player Rocky Cagnoni warns "if you lose the sight, you lose the fight." A great way to suppress a player posted on you, even if they are keeping a steady stream of paint in the air, is to outthink him with a clever snapshooting maneuver. He expects you to snap out of the same side of your bunker time and again, so

Footwork counts: don't trip over yourself!

throw a curveball: snap over the top of your bunker (or the other side if you are behind a too-tall standup) and shoot a quick burst at him.

Snap down quickly, as most of their team will have a shot on you when you pop over the top. Immediately snap to the side and shoot a stream at your opponent. This lightning-fast move puts him back into his bunker from the first stream, and catches him on his way back out of the bunker with your second stream. Even if you miss him completely, you have now regained control of that area and can post or suppress him with impunity.

Look for targets of opportunity, such as hoppers, barrels, and ankles. Watch the gaps between bunkers, and the edges of bunkers for when players carelessly back out from behind cover. Hoppers dance enticingly above low bunkers, and when a player sticks his barrel through an obstacle to shoot at your teammates, you can take a shot at the exposed barrel!

Shoot to suppress a move when you shoot to suppress an aggressive player. Rumbling a bunker and sending several shots around the sides is an effective way to keep his head down, but you should also know how to suppress a lane so the player will not be able to dart into a new bunker. Determine which bunker the player will move to, such as a thirty yard can from a back field standup, and keep a steady stream of paint through the lane that intersects the route he needs to take to make the bunker.

Experienced players seldom move when they see this steady stream of paint in their lane. Less experienced players normally move anyway, and your stream will eliminate them. Use this tactic off the break, or early in a game when players are making sudden moves. Together with normal suppressive fire techniques, shooting to suppress a move will totally shut down their ability to take new bunkers.

This tactic keeps players out of key bunkers such as the head of a snake, a bunker within arm's reach of the flag, etc. Often times keeping them out of key bunkers while your team settles into an offensive posture is as important as eliminating them straightaway. One opponent in a "key" bunker can swing the game...lane to keep them out of there!

Use cover noise to advance with less likelihood of detection. Woodsball players are attuned to hear opponents shuffling around. Nullify this by moving when the wind rustles leaves and grass, thus creating natural noise that your footsteps fade into. The wind also helps garble your conversations, so when you are in close proximity to opponents, give orders and instructions to teammates when the wind gusts around you to prevent your conversation from tipping off your opponents!

Keep in the action the whole game. Are you shooting at opponents who are actually in range? Are you being shot at by anyone? Are you covertly infiltrating their perimeter, or crawling unseen from bunker to bunker for a better angle? If you are not moving, shooting, or being shot at, you are not in the action and may as well not be playing! Paintball is a fast-paced game where every player counts, and you only count if you are doing something for your team! Move up until paint starts splattering around you, and then engage!

Running out of paint is a problem that should be addressed by wearing a good harness with plenty of pods. If you find yourself out of paint on the field, remember that live players can hand paint to you if you can get it from them. If not, just shoot air. Turn the anti-chop eye off if you carry an electro, and rap away as if you were actually playing. It takes a while for folks to realize that you are just dry firing! This buys time for your teammates to advance.

Stay in the action, even if you run out of air or paint. Calling yourself out hurts your team as much as you being shot out, and there is still plenty that you can do to help even if your marker is down. Your opponents will try to shoot you, and they will avoid running your way, even if your marker is down—it is human nature to avoid someone who is trying to shoot them, even if he is technically unable to get a ball out of the muzzle. By distracting them and giving them another player to deal with, you take some of the heat off of your teammates. Many tournaments give points to players who are still "alive" at the end of the game, making you worth points if you can just dodge paint for another few minutes. Also, you deny your opponents the points for eliminating you.

Act as a spotter for your team, or run paint to other players if you are out of air or your marker is down. You can hand off paint so long as you are still an active player. Call out the locations of your opponents, and act as the eyes and ears for your team. Actively watch the game, and hold your ground: your mere presence will often be enough to scare opponents into keeping their distance…so long as you refrain from making the mistake of screaming "I'm out of ____!"

Use a codeword that tells your team you are no longer capable of shooting. This way they know not to count on you for cover fire.

Being a non-playing player at this point affords you certain freedom—you no longer have to worry about eliminating players, so you can focus on the flag. Maneuver yourself into position to pull the flag, or to make a mad dash to hang the flag.

Don't drop your marker—the rules say that you have to carry your marker with you at all times on the field, lest you be called eliminated, so don't just lay it down and run off on a mission!

Leave firefights to squads; they aren't ideal for individuals. Remember your principal advantages as an individual: stealth and surprise. Both are compromised if you start shooting madly.

Most snipers and sneaky players find themselves vastly outnumbered, where advertising their position by spraying off a burst would do little more than bring unwanted attention. Instead, remember to take one shot at a time, and crawl away from large groups that are searching for you. Let the other players on your team charge ahead and fling paint for an hour…a sneaky player's role is too important and subtle for such noisy and overt action.

Fatal funnel. Though this term normally applies to door breaching procedures, it can also be applied readily to describe the action in the middle of the field. Ever notice how players in the middle of the field take balls from straight ahead as well as both sides? Try a strategy where you send a majority of players down a certain tapeline with only a small number of players in the middle. A few good players can hold off your opponents in the middle while giving the stacked tapeline suppressive cover. Use your tapeline players for the direct attack, and back door them once you breach their offensive line!

Help the referee pull eliminated players. When you hit an opponent, and actually see your mark on him, it is within your right to request that a referee check the player. Help him make the call quickly and accurately by clearly indicating which player you hit, and where you hit him, so the referee knows exactly where to look for your paint.

Protect your front player from being bunkered by keeping an eye on any opponent who is in position to bunker him. Use a reverse-cross-up formation (where you are behind your front player, and one of you looks to the left while the other looks to the right) to keep an eye on the part of your player's bunker that he has his back toward. If anyone tries to run around that side, shoot them.

When a bunkering move is coming, but you cannot see the opponents' bunker clearly, put a stream of suppressive fire around the side of your front player's bunker far enough away that he cannot accidentally lean into the stream and get hit.

Dig an opponent out of a tough bunker by out-thinking him. Look at which side he pops out from most, and then send a barrage of paint to, and just past, the other side of the bunker. Occasionally toss a single round past his favorite side. When he thinks you're suppressing the other side, he becomes inclined to lean out his favored side of the bunker…right into that lone, hard-to-detect paintball. Being smarter than he, you actually forced this behavior and are ready to send a stream right into his goggles if you don't get him with the stray shots. Lead them into the trap!

Read your hits. When playing a bunker, you should only get hit in the front of the marker, your trailing shoulder (the one your tank is against), your hands, and your goggles, as these are the only parts of you that should be exposed during snapshooting. After each game, think about where you got hit, and where the opponent was when he shot you.

Hits on your foot or pack tell you to keep your entire body behind cover. Hits to your body indicate that either you are leaning too far out during snapshooting, or you are not using your bunker properly as a shield against laterally oriented opponents. You only get hit when you do something wrong, so studying the hits helps you figure out what mistakes not to make next time!

Bring along your camera and a blaze orange vest. Set your marker aside for a game, and with the referee's permission, walk onto the field with your vest, goggles, and camera. Follow the action from the tapelines, or on forested fields, wander freely around the field and take pictures of your team and your opponents. While enjoying the freedom of being a spectator, pay attention to how the field plays and where different groups go on maneuvers. Look at which moves work, which ones don't, and why.

You can pay closer attention to the orientation and composition of bunkers, and gain a better concept of the game in progress, when not under the stress of playing and being shot at. After a while you develop a second sense about where big plays are going to happen, and where you need to be to get the great action photos. This correlates directly to a player's sense of where action is, and where they need to go to get in the game. The skills carry over very well between photographer and player. As you move with your camera and impunity, you'll develop a preternatural sense for the game.

Paintball is as much a mind game as it is an athletic one, and your biggest opponent is yourself. The right attitudinal approach can mean the difference between victory and failure much more so than any gadget you could ever buy…and your state of mind is free.

The basic rule of paintball is that players are eliminated by one break. Thus, the twenty balls per second coming your way are nineteen more than the guy needs: and the one ball in your chamber is all you need, so long as you truly believe that you can put that one shot on your opponent. No matter the age, size, gender, gear, or experience of your opponents, you all shoot at the same velocity and fall to the same one break rule.

Believe in yourself, and stay true to your instincts and the moves you practice…you never have to let yourself down.

DRILLS

Better practice makes better players. There are all sorts of gizmos you can buy for your markers, but few will markedly improve your game. So, too, with training: there are all sorts of ways to screw around on a field, but only some of them actually improve your skills. These exercises are used by pro teams, at paintball skill camps, and by amateur teams throughout the country. Run your team through some of the drills and see a difference. Run them through all the drills on a regular basis, and see a lot of gold medals.

Triangle drill. Reportedly invented by Bob Long's Ironmen, and taught to the author by Total Greif, this drill involves three bunkers, three players, and six soda cans. The goal of this exercise is to teach snapshooting speed and accuracy, while forcing participants to play tight in their bunkers.

Arrange any three bunkers in a triangular formation, where each is equally spaced from the other. Place one soda can at each "side" of the bunker where a wayward foot would be if a player hiding on the outside of the triangle got careless. Each player now has two cans by his bunker, and can see one can by each of the other two bunkers (one a right hand shot, one a left hand shot).

At "go!" each player snapshoots his opponents' cans. Only after hitting the can is he allowed to shoot the player. Normal paintball rules apply, as one hit anywhere on a player or his gear results in an elimination. Bunkering is not allowed. The last player in the game is the winner.

This drill strongly reinforces the need for first-shot accuracy when played with pumps, and seriously improves snapshooting speed when played with lightning-quick electronic markers.

Accurately run-and-gun. Few moves are as difficult to execute effectively as accurate running and shooting. Some players sacrifice speed for accuracy and volume of paint in the air while others up their speed with a predictable loss of effectiveness. Both can be improved through proper training in the art of running and shooting.

For solo practice, gather an empty paintball case and a metal stake (the kind used to post ropes around fields, hold up snow fences, etc) or a suitable stick or dowel rod. Post the box at about chest height in the middle of a "lane," where a player would presumably run off the break. Walk to the opposite start station. On your own "go!" turn and charge to your first bunker while shooting at that box. The first time you probably won't hit it at all…keep trying. Go slowly until you get the hang of aiming without being able to sight down the barrel, running in a hunched over and uncomfortable position, etc. Increase your speed as your accuracy improves.

For team practices, break players into groups of two, with one group at each start station. One group focuses on running to tapeline bunkers while the other group drills on shooting. On "go!" the shooters turn and engage the runners.

For new players with little experience in the art of the run-and-gun, start by running the team through the box drill, as it reinforces the behavior of shooting one fixed spot in a lane instead of getting distracted by movement and shooting where the player appears to be (which is no where near where they will be by the time those slow paintballs get downfield). Then work them slowly towards shooting at moving targets, giving them a few mandatory turns as runners to help get them over any fear about being shot.

Target shoot. Instead of wasting all their paint at the chrono station on dinky targets and whirling widgets, have your teammates find an empty field and set up soda cans, water bottles, and other random, inexpensive targets. Place them on the ground next to a bunker like a foot accidentally slipped out from behind cover, or a hand carelessly swung wide while grabbing a pod. Put targets in line with holes in the bunkers to give the challenge of shooting between logs or through gaps in pallets.

Now get into position behind bunkers and snapshoot these targets! Once you eliminate one or two targets, power your way into another bunker by shooting suppressive fire at another target;

snapshoot it if you missed on the run. Engage more targets, and repeat the move until you clear the field. Reset the targets and get your teammates into it…it's fun, a great way to exercise an itchy trigger finger, and improves your shooting skill enormously!

Stick target. This drill involves a volunteer, a stick, and an old rag. It's easy to set up but hard to master. Take a three foot long stick, broom handle, etc, and wrap an old towel around one end. Tape the cloth in place. Send one teammate downfield (with goggles on, of course) to hide behind a complicated bunker, such as a Hyperball octopus or in the middle of an Ultimate AirBall snake. To present the target, he sticks the padded end of the stick out from the sides of the bunker, the top of the bunker, and everywhere else, keeping the target visible for three seconds at a time.

The shooter needs to hide behind a bunker and snapshoot at irregular intervals (remember that rhythm can be anticipated by your opponent and will be used against you!), engaging the target every time he sees it. This drill mimics what it is like to see a foot, hand, elbow, hopper, or other part of a player for just a second as they shift around behind their bunkers. Learn how to make your first shot count while snapshooting against a small target that is only exposed for a split second, and you'll be completely unstoppable.

Ghost walking. Formerly taught at the famous Ronn Stern Camps by legendary player and instructor Mike Paxson, this will sharpen your wits better than most other drills. One player starts at the "far end" of a field, in a large bunker that completely hides him, although everyone knows where he is. That player has a marker and lots of paint…but no one else does. At "go!" your entire team charges from the opposing start station and takes up their first bunkers. The purpose of this drill: for each player to tag the shooter's bunker without getting shot. Sound tough? It is. So is paintball.

Players learn to move when the shooter is engaging other players…he can only shoot at one player at a time, the same as any opponent. While he shoots at the left tapeline players, the right tapeline players have a golden opportunity to advance. When he reloads, everyone should advance a bunker or two. While part of the bunker obscures his vision of a certain area of field, anyone who is in his "blind spot" needs to move pronto! This drill helps players see these subtle opportunities, these fleeting windows where they can advance without detection…perfect for gaining ground without getting hit, and ideal for seeing the opportunities they need to bunker players.

Run through drill. Once a tapeline is blown open, players need to capitalize immediately to perform a "run through," the move where a player penetrates the skirmish line and side-shoots as many opponents as he can while swinging around to their back-field and looking for angles to shoot the rest of their team in the back. When properly executed, this move can eliminate fully half or more of the opposing team with the potential loss of only one of your players…and the crowds love it. This move involves elements of the run-and-gun, as well as the target-seeking skills of a woodsball player. Run through moves are executed in both woodsball and speedball!

Take empty barrels, or empty paint cases suspended on stakes, and place them randomly behind bunkers so that they are completely invisible from a head-on angle. Your players then take turns running down alternating tapelines, searching for the targets and eliminating them. Some targets should be close enough to require bunkering, while players have to long-ball others from across the width of the field. You should encourage speed as well as accuracy, while coaching your players to call the codeword for "run through" before engaging, and making sure that they stay low to present as small of a moving target as possible.

Bunkering drill. Put a target behind a bunker, and have three players engage the bunker. Each of the three players will take turns bunkering the target, while the other two players provide cover fire from midfield bunkers. This drill helps players get into the basic mindset of charging a "live" bunker while their friends shoot suppressive fire all around them. It also helps insert and back players learn the timing and aiming necessary to keep a bunker suppressed, while not shooting their own player when he moves to bunker the opponent.

To spice up these drills, send a teammate to a position near the "target" bunker and have him shoot suppressive fire towards the players running the drill. The shooter should be declared untouchable, and no one should shoot at him...his role is solely to provide incentive to play bunkers tightly and effectively, step lively, and shoot accurately. Engaging static targets at great length while envisioning a game is great, but when folks start to slack off, there's nothing like instant paint-mark feedback to get the drill back on track!

MANEUVERS

These general formations, maneuvers, and team tactics are effective in scenario games as well as open play, with many effective as speedball strategy. With creative modification and an understanding of the sport's dynamics, the same maneuver or tactical concept can apply across the board!

Skirmish Push. This is the default maneuver used in most every open play game, and the tactic reverted to when all else fails.

Every player runs forward until they get shot at, or get scared, whichever comes first. You can harness the power of this basic behavior by giving the classic call "charge!" and inciting a World War I blitz on the skirmish line. Though it only gives you 50/50 odds, the basic skirmish push is the most encountered offense on the field and deserves the respect due its popularity.

Study it in action, and watch how some players charge farther and faster than others. Watch how some players show leadership initiative, and where the players seem to cluster. Use this basic strategy of "let's just go get 'em" to read how a field plays during the first game or two of the day, and then base your grand strategy upon the information you gather watching the basic skirmish play out—you can also spot leaders among the players, and use them to execute special missions and maneuvers later in the day.

Sneaky Pete. This is a woodsball equivalent of a speedball run through, only involving stealth rather than blazing speed. While your opponents are busy engaging your team on one section of field, fall well back from the skirmish line and charge to the quieter tapeline or other area of the field where you do not hear any action. When playing a large field, ask teammates returning from reinsertions or hanging out in the backfield about where you can find a lack of opposition. Go there, being aware of your changing position relative to the conflict.

Your goal is to approach the action from the side: as players engage opponents head on, they often ignore what is to their side. Go "behind the lines" and then find side angles. Approach from the side, and slightly behind...right where they would never expect you. Flashy players will charge as soon as their position is compromised, as they seldom can stay in the game for long when completely surrounded. This diminishes the havoc they can wreak, but affords their team a window of opportunity to charge while the opponents try to engage, and hide from, threats in two different directions. Good Sneaky Petes will engage their targets sparingly, hiding and causing as much damage as possible before they are compromised.

Thief. For Sneaky Pete players who have no ambition to take on an entire team single-handedly, they can become "thieves" with much the same technique. Once you disappear into the foliage, make your way swiftly to the opponents' end of the field. Search for their base, and approach it from behind. Crawl into position behind their flag station, and very slowly, very quietly, steal their flag without shooting. Now, retreat with equal stealth, taking their flag with you.

Beware that now you will be sneaking towards your own teammates, and might get confused for one of your own opponents! Call out your team affiliation to any player that you see facing you: they are likely your own players! Any player that has their back to you is likely an opponent, so avoid contact with them, barrel tag them, or shoot them once in the back if you must. Often times your opponents will just let you go if they see you moving in their same direction, assuming that you are on their team!

Bunkering is essentially player-on-player flanking, a personal adaptation of the classic group maneuver

Flanking. This basic move is executed when your team blows a tapeline open, or maneuvers a detachment to the side of your objective. While the bulk of your team engages opponents from the front, your teammates engage your opponents from the side, exploiting the fact that most bunkers do not have effective protection against side angles.

This maneuver can eliminate a large amount of players in a short amount of time, and is another one of the intuitive moves that you find individuals executing automatically. Focus that tendency into a small group maneuver, and your team will annihilate the opposition.

The Shocker. Combine elements of a baited ambush with some diversionary tactics. Recruit your Sneaky Pete players. Destroy the opposition.

Curl your ring finger toward the base of your hand, and hold it there with your thumb. This makes The Shocker, a tactic you should know like the back of your hand. Your pinky is the Shocker Team, while your forefinger and middle fingers are the bulk of your team. Divide players in a 3:1 or 4:1 ratio, with the fewer players being the quieter, bolder, more disciplined players you need on the Shocker Team.

At the start signal, immediately move the bulk of your players toward the skirmish line, or opponents' base. If you divide the field in half lengthwise, this group should be entirely on one side of the field, and as far away from the centerline as it makes tactical sense to move them. They will engage the opponents fiercely, and should choose bunkers that offer protection from the open side of the field as well as protection from the opponents in front of them.

The Shocker Team should move to the opposite side of the field at game on, keeping parallel to the main force but staying as quiet as possible and not shooting. There should be a good amount of open ground between the mass and the Shocker Team, as you are creating a corridor in which to trap your opponents. Once opponents appear, the entire Shocker Team should hide and remain silent. In short order, intrepid opponents will stream out of the base or away from the conflict and attempt a basic flanking maneuver against your players. To do this, they will flood the corridor, and put their backs to the Shocker Team. Now, give 'em The Shocker!

During the ensuing chaos, two of your Sneaky Pete players should peel away from the Shocker Team and disappear along the tapeline and behind the opponents' position. They can steal the flag, eliminate the general, otherwise win the game or capture points for the objective.

A second benefit of this move is that the opponents who flood the corridor will come from one side of the engagement, likely leaving that entire flank open…after all, they thought it was secure and they could move to flank your team! The irony is that you are using their tactics against them.

Bait. Snipers use bait to lure players into clearings where they can shoot the unsuspecting schmuck. Small groups can use the exact same tactic to eliminate large numbers of opponents. Bring a prop onto the field, such as an empty box wrapped in gold colored paper, and place it along a heavily used trail. Alternatively, you can dress a player in non-paintball clothes (such as a cheap suit from a thrift store) and make him stand in the open without a marker, acting like he's an important informant, trader, etc. The possibilities are endless, but the point is the same: play upon the curiosity of a player or group to lure them into an ambush.

You can also beat a trail through the underbrush, and then stage two players at the head of this new trail. When they see opponents coming, they should noisily and obviously move down the new trail, teasing opponents to follow them. This will take opponents off on an irrelevant chase—or straight into your ambush—while their team suffers the lack of support during vital missions.

Bait And Switch. Without violating any rules about hiding flags or transporting props, simply misdirect opponents. When defending a base, prop, flag, or person, find a different base out of sight (but not too far away, in case you are opposing local players or players with maps) from the real location of the desired object. Arrange bunkers so that this base looks more important than the "real" one you need to defend, and then defend it with a majority of your players.

Hang a t-shirt from a branch in the center, mimicking a flag. Set an intriguing prop somewhere in the base so opponents can see it from somewhat far away—props that have "expired" (their point value has been calculated, and they are no longer worth anything) are ideal for this decoy work.

The idea is to bait a convincing-looking objective, and then dupe them into thinking it is what they're after…thus switching their focus from the real objective to the fake one. Be sure that you tell the referees about the ruse so that they don't get suckered into believing it too!

Tapeline Push. Blowing a tapeline open is critical to swinging a skirmish line sideways, exploiting the weaknesses of front-protection-only bunkers and forcing opponents into the crossfire between your and your teammates' angles. Opening a gap along a tapeline facilitates a flanking maneuver. Flooding this opening with players can swing a game quickly to your favor.

Move the bulk of your players to one tapeline, leaving only a few to guard the center of the field and the opposite tapeline. This large group charges along the tapeline, engaging opponents and relying on speed and shock value to advance where lesser-power moves would result in stagnation. Once the group breaks through the skirmish line, they flank while simultaneously pushing deeper. Think of a net spreading across the field, pushing opponents to the back corner of their side, and you will understand the basic concept of the tapeline push.

Run Through. Front players normally perform run through moves, the flashy moves that find them behind the skirmish line shooting opponents in the side and back. Get your front players in position behind large front bunkers that can shield their forward movement from a majority of the field; snakes usually work quite well for this purpose. Once they clear the field in front of them by eliminating their closest opponent, they run past the first and second lines of offensive players before making a ninety-degree turn to run towards the opposite tapeline. Run throughs can be used to clear an area near a tapeline so that a corridor opens for players to twist the skirmish line sideways, or they can serve to eliminate many opponents from the center of the field.

The key to executing a run through is timing: players must "survive" the initial charge through the skirmish line, and then take the opposing side by surprise. Execute a run through after dropping a critical opponent or bunkering a front player.

Bunker Buster. Imagine trying to stop the raging flood when a dam breaks...you can't do it. Not even close. That is exactly what you must do to your opponents: overrun, overwhelm, and overtake them with force and precision. Massive World War I-style battle-field charges work, but not as well as more focused attacks.

Have teammates form a tight cluster, with only two feet separating each player front to back, side to side. Gather enough players so that you have at least three layers, an outside layer of players who carry fast shooting markers and realize they will be hit, a middle layer of players who are equally fearless, and a center mass of players who know how to spread out and shoot opponents in the back once they break through a skirmish line or into a fortress.

Have the rest of your players in the area shoot massive amounts of suppressive fire at the fortress or skirmish line around where you want to breach, and then immediately send the bunker busting group charging ahead at full speed. The outside players will get hit in the chaos, likely numerous times, and should cease the charge when eliminated, as per the rules. Be sure they know to run out of the way of their stampeding teammates so as to not slow down the charge as they peel away and head to the reinsertion zones.

With the combined firepower of the group and support players, the group should be able to penetrate the embattlements with a good number of players left. Now, they go deeper and spread out to side- and back- shoot their opponents.

Gauntlet. This move involves flooding both tapelines with players, such that your fastest players on each side secure as much side-field real estate as they can while leaving the middle open. Your slower players should stick to the tapelines as well, pointing their markers toward the center. Leave a strong contingent of players in the backfield to close the distance between the rearmost tapeline players. Now you have a long staple-shaped formation on the field, with the bottom closed so opponents cannot charge through the middle to raid your flag station.

Beginners naturally gravitate toward areas of the field with less action, and many advanced players go there looking for opportunities to flank or sneak behind the lines. In this case, that area is the corridor between columns of your team…where your opponents will soon find themselves in crossfire! Players cannot simultaneously engage opponents in front and behind them, which means that any opponent who charges into the open space between your tapeline players will get shot.

Move the formation downfield until your team surrounds the entire opposing team, or one of your tapeline players can steal their flag and run down the safe corridor between teammates and the tapeline all the way back to your base!

Classic Wedge. Allocate your players so that the fastest are in the middle of the field and the slowest are on the tapelines. Have every player charge downfield at the go signal, stopping only when they start taking paint. The resulting distribution of players resembles a V, with your front players at the skirmish line. As they break through the skirmish line, the whole V should shift downfield to get your players in position for side shots on the opposing team.

The Classic Wedge formation is evident at the break, with two tape runners, and three mid players in the center, shooting lanes

Red Herring. Scenario games are all about time management: objectives are worth points if they are held for specific periods of time, after which they generally become worthless…for a while, at least. Effective leaders make schedules of when each objective "expires," and coordinate attacks so that their team controls the objectives at the necessary time. Critical to controlling the objective is maneuvering players into position, which is where this tactic comes in handy.

Defending teams should take a detachment of players sufficient to engage an enormous amount of opponents, but not so numerous as to leave the point-value objective poorly guarded. This intrepid detachment of dispensable players should strike off towards the opponents' position, moving toward areas of the field where no objectives are located. Along the way they should send two to four players to antagonize the opponents, leading them to the red herring group.

The red herring players need to find a fortified position that appears to be of some importance, and then defend it intensely. Choose a position that is near to one of your team's reinsertion points if the diversion needs to last for longer than one reinsertion period; otherwise, players should be instructed to reinsert as close to the actual objective as they can.

The red herring group engages their opponents as fiercely as possible, miring the entire opposing division in one place far away from where they need to be. This "objective" has no value, so the skirmish is largely pointless…but few paintball players can walk past a raging battle without joining in! The more opponents you distract, the easier it will be for your team to defend the real objective!

Wingman. This small group maneuver uses deception to destroy units and secure bases. Three players approach a fortified position, with one player slipping off out of sight to the side just before the group makes contact. The remaining players dig in and engage the fortification head on, creating significant noise and disruption. The wingman sneaks around the side of the position and maneuvers his way behind the opposing players. While the opponents are occupied with the diversion in front of them, he shoots each player one time in the back. Any players that turn to shoot, after being shot, get shot a second time.

Let 'Em Come. This move involves keeping a majority, or all, of your team at your flag station to defend against the opponents. It is generally a very poor idea, though can be deployed in this redeeming variation: send three players downfield, along the tapelines, with orders not to engage any opponents. These players should lay low and let their opponents run past them.

Once the threat is gone, they should run to the opposing flag station, steal the flag, and return, swinging wide around the rear of their own base to enter through a pre-decided "safe corridor" area so they don't receive friendly fire. As often as the basic tactic of staying behind is suggested, it should be shot down; only when all control of the group is lost should you agree that "yeah, everyone staying back here sounds like a great idea!" It's understandable if then you are the first tape runner to charge and try this maneuver!

Zigzag. Think of this move as a massive leap frog tactic, where two lines of offensive players help each other push the skirmish line back into your opponents' territory. Your team charges the skirmish line abreast, as if executing the basic skirmish push maneuver. A second line of front players forms one row of bunkers back, and calls out the positions of opponents. If you draw a line from one player to another, you see a zigzag pattern.

On a pre-arranged signal, every player pops up and engages their nearest opponent; the rear line of players run-and-gun toward a line of bunkers one row in front of their own offensive line, powering themselves in. The new rear line advances in turn, leapfrogging en masse.

Hounding. Generally considered a dirty move, this tactic nonetheless has viable applications. Locate the reinsertion point for your opponents, and move a small detachment of snipers or very stealthy players to "secure" it. Most game formats do not allow for capturing a reinsertion point, though if permitted, capturing them has tremendous effect. If you cannot officially "capture" the reinsertion point, post your players around it in such a way as to be able to destroy the entire force when they come streaming out during reinsertion.

These hiding players would be well advised to encamp in two distinct and separate areas, so that should the reinserting players get a foothold or other opponents arrive to assist in eliminating the snipers, only one part of your ambush force will be wiped out, leaving the other to wreak havoc upon the next reinsertion.

When tactical units are not available for this role, use radio-equipped snipers. Order them to radio troop movements and positions to their central command and only shoot point-value officers or important leaders.

Sever. While walking the field, pay attention to trails and how the landscape dictates the flow of the action. Take notice of which trails and paths are likely to convey large numbers of players from a reinsertion point to a critical base, and which ones might be well traveled by central command staff as they move between critical objectives. Assign special groups to find these paths and encamp on them, keeping any players and tanks from passing through the area. This can serve to keep medics from reaching the action, as well as keeping central command staff mired in irrelevant positions while their leadership falls apart in their absence.

Sever supplies, tanks, important players, prop carriers, and medics from the rest of the force.

In recball, you can use this tactic to keep opponents from crossing a bridge or using a trail. A small number of players can shut down a vital part of the field while the rest of your open play group follows another trail or path. This will largely do away with the need to leave any stragglers behind to guard the flag, freeing up manpower for special units and the main attack force!

MONEY

You have to pay to play, and money can get very tight, very fast. Follow these ideas to work sponsorships, raise private funds, and save money!

Pay by credit card or check whenever possible. Sit down every December with your year's worth of credit card statements and cancelled checks, and total how much you spent on paintball that year. Cancelled checks and credit card statements make this accounting easy. Inflate your total by 15% to cover all the cash-transactions you made, the associated costs of gas and food that you probably don't have receipts for, and to put a little money toward "bigger and better things" for next year. The resulting figure is how much money you should budget for paintball in the coming year. Remember, you are not trying to guilt-trip yourself about how much you spent, just trying to figure out how much you need to set aside.

Get a job at the field. Most field owners let employees play for free, or a steeply discounted rate, and offer them special deals on air and paint as well. Work the wholesale angle by asking the field owner if you can order a number of cases of paint, or other gear, through the field to get wholesale pricing.

Look for group discounts. Many fields offer discounts for groups, and some offer perks like free play for the official "group organizer." Do a little legwork to promote a day at the field, get your friends to drive there together, and rightfully present yourself as the group organizer.

Bulk rate. Ask about discounts on paint and markers for buying three, five, or even ten at a time. Get friends to pool their money to split an order of paint, or for other gear: find folks who all need goggles, markers, etc, at the same time and put together a group order. This also helps standardize the gear your group uses, so that you can swap replacement parts and know exactly how to fix each others' markers when they go down.

Compare prices on everything, and keep in mind the benefit of buying locally. The internet offers great deals on just about any gear you need, but the shipping expenses chew up your total savings. Local stores and fields have varying prices, so shop around before purchasing, and then choose the store that has the right gear at the right price.

Consider the follow-up service as part of the price. What warranties does the store, field, or internet site offer? Most stores will gladly work on a marker they sold you, often charging very little or nothing...but if you bring in a marker that you bought elsewhere, they slap on expensive hourly fees. Many stores give you coupon books, field passes, and other goodies when you purchase a marker or tank from them...this is a very good deal for you, and should be reflected in your final decision on where to buy a certain piece of gear.

Though great deals exist on the internet, the core benefit of buying gear locally is that your money supports a store or field that you can rely on. Every dollar you spend at the local field helps them stay open, and each purchase at the local pro shop helps keep them available to you as a source of emergency parts and expert service.

Get sponsored. Many teams try to get sponsored, but few succeed. The key to getting noticed by sponsors is to make your team visible. Submit a written introduction to the team and request for sponsorship to the public relations manager of the intended sponsor. Include photographs of your team, one paragraph biographies on each player, a history of the tournaments or other events you played, a list of any trophies or Sportsmanship Awards you won, a short essay on what you seek from them and another on what you will do for them in return.

Companies look for teams that have been around for awhile, so don't expect a team less than one year old to pick up much in the way of sponsorship. They also look for track records that include important tournament victories and Sportsmanship Awards or similar honors. Be sure to include photocopies of any newspaper or magazine articles on your team or the events you compete in, as sponsors are interested in teams that make names for themselves.

The key to seeing money is giving your sponsors a return on every check they write you. What will you do for the money? The minimum expectation of sponsors is that you put their logo on your uniform. Beyond that, you can take their logo merchandise (key chains, Frisbees, t-shirts, etc) to tournaments and give it to fans to help promote your sponsor's business.

Offer to hand out coupons or flyers at local events, and ask if the establishment has any banners or signs you can take to tournaments. If you get a team photo published in a newspaper or magazine, display your sponsor's banner in your team photo and then submit a clipping of the article as a thank-you to the sponsor.

Volunteer the team's service to work charity events for the sponsor, such as staffing the tables during a bake sale or selling raffle tickets for a community auction. This helps the sponsor, gives your team more time to hang out together, and helps you get more money for paintball!

Fields like sponsoring their "home team," and with these sponsorships come valuable discounts on play, paint, and air...and often the expectation that your team will referee open play, perform field maintenance, hand out flyers, and actively bring new players to the facility.

Manufacturers generally want teams to use their gear exclusively, which can create friction among players. Marker sponsorships, where you receive discounts or free markers, are as divisive as they are wonderful: players are particularly fond of their personal markers, and generally do not like giving them up in favor of the "team marker." With sponsorships they must.

Whatever the sponsor makes, you better be sure to use, even if they did not sponsor you with their gloves, goggles, etc, and you have to buy them separately. Should a sponsor make pants, for example, you should not be seen in public or in the media wearing any other company's pants; but if the sponsor only makes pants, you can wear whatever goggles you want. The idea is to avoid conflicts of representation, where you use (and thus, endorse) gear by your sponsor's competitor—that's a surefire way to lose your sponsorship!

Generate publicity for your sponsors whenever possible. Should you have an equipment sponsorship, review the product objectively by thoroughly testing it during practices and events. If your team starts using the product, submit a review, pictures, and photocopies of raw data (such as a log of velocity readings from a chronograph, chart of group size for accuracy, etc) to a paintball magazine. If it gets printed, your sponsors will be thrilled, your team gets a major mention in a publication, and everyone benefits from your initiative.

Sponsors are all around you, from your home field to the local pizza shop. Many regional teams have little to offer international companies, but can do wonders for promoting local establishments. Independently owned establishments are your best bets for local sponsorship.

Corporately owned franchises, such as chain restaurants and retail stores, often cannot make decisions on sponsoring sporting teams without approval from someone hundreds of miles away who will just throw away your proposal…but locally owned businesses make their decisions in-house, and you can usually get your proposal to the owner or manager without having it lost in a paper shuffle.

Feel free to shoot for the moon and submit sponsorship requests to major paintball companies, but you are advised to build a solid base of local support and a solid track record of success and exposure before approaching companies that routinely field hundreds of requests from teams that play in the professional leagues and notable amateur tournaments. Start small, but never lose your focus on improving your game and expanding your sponsorships!

HEALTH

DEHYDRATION

Dehydration is the enemy of every paintball player and all other athletes! Scorching summer heat drains the fluid from your body, putting great stress on your tissues and leading to fatigue, exhaustion…even heat stroke and death. Many players don't realize, though, that they can get dehydrated just as easily in the dead of winter, comfortable spring or chilly fall.

Water is the original and best way to stay hydrated, and has worked to keep humans alive for the entirety of our existence. Soda has not. Sports drinks have only been around for a few decades, though science suggests the electrolytes (salt) contained in the drinks help keep our neurons firing right.

Replacing the electrolytes we lose while exercising, the reasoning states, improves the functioning of our muscles and brains. However, sugar is usually the second ingredient in sodas and sports drinks (and sometimes the third, fourth, and fifth ingredients as well). Sugar gives you quick energy that is just as quickly lost, leaving you prematurely tired just when you should be hitting your stride. Thus, sports drinks remain an emergency step to correct dehydration, but proper hydration with water is the best prevention. With an entire team shooting at you and hundreds of dollars invested in your gear and field passes, who wants to risk a health emergency?

Start drinking extra water at least one day before you play. The recommended daily water intake for an average adult is 64 ounces, which is half of a gallon…and soda actually counts against that amount! Drink at least this amount of water, spread throughout the day, prior to going out to play. Carry a water bottle around with you at the field, and the day before—if it's always in your hand, you'll always be tempted to drink out of it!

Warm water is absorbed into your blood and used by your body faster than cold water. Your body must heat the water to a usable temperature—around ninety eight degrees, your body's temperature—before it can be of much use to your cells. The less your body must heat the water, the faster it can be absorbed and hydrate you. Thus, room temperature water helps you faster than ice water, even if you don't like the taste ...

Beware of Hyponatremia, the condition where you over-hydrate and flush electrolytes out of your system. Symptoms of hyponatremia include headache, nausea, and generally feeling really ill. When you detect these symptoms, sit in the shade and have a friend seek medical assistance for you—you may just be overworked, but hyponatremia is a life-threatening condition that requires medical attention and only medical professionals can diagnose the difference.

Keep your water bottle and food out of the sun. Sun-heated water tastes unpleasant, and food can quickly spoil in direct sunlight. When you put your paintballs in the shade, spare a thought for your food! Taking two ice chests, one for paintballs (without ice in it, of course) and the other for your food, is a good way to keep tight environmental control on food and paint.

Carry a small bottle of water in an empty slot in your pack, as the 0.5 liter bottles are roughly the same diameter as a tube. Drink between games, in safe areas where it's OK to raise your mask. Drink at least 64 ounces of water the day of the event, and a bit more is better.

Invest in a hydration pack you can wear on your back if you find yourself playing long games, such as scenarios and big games. The Camelback system, as well as the Intersept Akwapac (tested and used by the author) are solid choices, and can be outfitted with pouches for tubes (the Akwapac comes with pouches specifically for this use).

The key feature, besides a large water reservoir, of these packs is that they include a flexible drinking tube that wraps around your body to clip onto your shoulder or collar. Specially designed nozzles on the tube slip right under your goggles so you can drink from the pack without disturbing your goggles or shifting your body very much. Most importantly, they provide a relatively hands-free way of staying healthy during the rigors of our rugged sport!

FOOD

Pack a light lunch when going to fields that lack dining facilities. The field gourmet can take an AC converter for the cigarette lighter in their car and use an electric grill or other small appliance to make hamburgers for your team, or to power a hotplate for soup and coffee on cold days. Lighter foods, such as cold cut sandwiches, fresh fruits and vegetables, and energy bars, make great meals. Greasy foods, which unfortunately include the hotdogs and hamburgers popular at many fields, slow you down and make your stomach uneasy when you run in the rising heat.

Avoid packing any food with mayonnaise or similar condiments that can spoil quickly. Individual serving packages of BBQ sauce, horseradish, ketchup and mustard make great pack-along condiments that are generally still good when not refrigerated.

When making the perfect sandwich for the field, rolling the best burrito for later, or making any other food that has to sit for a few hours while you play, remember to keep moist ingredients (tomatoes, lettuce) separate from absorbent ingredients (bread, tortillas). Pack these basic ingredients separately in your cooler to keep tomato juice and condensation from turning your hearty bread into disgusting mush.

INSECTS

Put something over the lid of your soda can or water bottle, or a paper towel over your sandwich, to keep out the sweat bees, hornets, and flies. Think it hurts to get bunkered? Swallow an angry hornet sometime …

Prevent bites from ticks, chiggers, and other nasty little forest bugs while you go crawling through their natural environment. While chiggers are mainly an itchy nuisance, ticks can carry a range of diseases including the dreaded Lyme Disease. You can prevent the illnesses and discomfort these bugs bring by spraying your gear and the cuffs (inside and out) on the legs and wrists of your clothing. Also spray around the collar, waistband, and the lower edge of shirts. Roll your cuffs and collars up, and spray on the inside part to form a barrier against any bugs that crawl inside of your clothes.

Use a Premethrin or Permagone spray for this, keeping the chemicals away from bare skin. For your skin, use a skin-safe bug spray with Deet or other powerful chemicals. The skin-safe sprays deter bugs from crawling on you, while the Premethrin kills any that make their way onto or under your clothes.

Lyme Disease? Is there a red, irritated circle around a tick bite you sustained recently? This could be an indication of Lyme Disease, so check with a physician immediately before you develop a potentially deadly fever. Any random fever in the days following being in the forest could be a sign of an insect-born illness in your body, and you should seek a medical evaluation to head off any problems. Simple antibiotics can take care of most of the illnesses.

Tick, leech, and other bites are annoying but easily dealt with. Remove the critter according to health provider instructions, and then circle that area of skin with a black permanent marker. This way you can remember exactly where the bite occurred, and monitor the spot for infection, irritation, swelling, and other indications that something is going wrong! When the mark wears off, so too has most of the threat from the bite.

PRE-GAME HEALTHCARE

Physical fitness and self confidence go hand in hand. Forget the mirror: a flat stomach, toned legs, the perfect tan…these are dumb, often unobtainable, ideals of perfection that we are hit with every day in the media. Physically fit individuals are capable of performing the physical tasks involved in their daily lives, don't get winded from taking the stairs, and generally enjoy good overall health. Your doctor—not billboards or glamour magazines— knows exactly what the physical fitness standards are for your body type, height, lifestyle, and family history… .

But there are important steps every paintball player should take to ensure their body is up to the rugged demands of intense paintball action!

Certain studies link physical fitness with confidence, favoring a positive relationship: those who are in good shape feel better about themselves, thus making it easier to go to the gym, do exercises at home, or otherwise lead healthy lifestyles. Conversely, those in poor shape tend to feel worse about themselves, with the counterintuitive drive to avoid improvement and remain trapped in a downward spiral of dwindling health and poor lifestyle decisions…just the same as those in good health fall into an upward spiral of feeling great and doing more to feel even better. There's not much of a middle ground …

Get the psychological and performance edge that you need to win by starting with a good foundation: a healthy body.

Lead your friends, squad, or team through simple stretches and a light cardio exercise the morning of game day. Remember how the day after a hard practice you hurt in muscles you never knew you had? You can prevent that by stretching in ways you never knew you needed too…but skip the field-side yoga and go with standard gym class warm-ups.

A good "workout burn" is alright, but pain is a sign that you're doing something gravely wrong! Stop immediately if anything hurts. After limbering up and stretching out, you will be able to bend and twist faster and more painlessly to dodge paintballs and hide behind the smallest bunkers…and you'll avoid injuries!

Do not bounce, as this can tear muscles and overstretch ligaments…favor instead a slow and steady stretch, and then a slow return to the standing position. Repeat these stretches several times.

Toe touches. Stand with your feet shoulder width apart and bend over to touch your toes. If you can touch your toes, flatten your fingers along the top of your feet until you can't bend any lower.

Arm stretches. Raise your right hand over your shoulder, then drop it down to scratch your back. Use your left hand to push lightly down on your right elbow, bending your arm down farther. Do this for your left arm as well, repeating several times while being very careful not to stress your shoulder unnecessarily.

Twists. Put your hands on your hips and twist as far to the left as you can twist, then twist to the right as far as you can go. Repeat, going slowly. This exercise is great to loosen your abdominal muscles for quick twisting to counter bunker moves, dodge paint, or to snap around your bunker!

Ankle grabs. Spread your feet slightly wider than shoulder width apart, and lean over to grab your left ankle with your right hand. Try to pull your upper body toward your ankle. Repeat with your left hand reaching for your right ankle.

Standing reach. Now pass your hands between your legs, grabbing for the grass behind you. Reach as far back as you can.

Sitting toe touches. Sit down, and extend your legs straight out in front of you. Keeping your back straight, reach your fingertips toward your toes. Try to grab your toes and pull them back toward your body, while trying to pull your head toward your knees. Be careful not to overdo it! Spread your legs wide, and reach straight forward toward where your feet just were.

Sitting ankle grabs. With your legs spread wide, reach your right hand towards your left ankle, then your left hand toward your right ankle.

Leg crosses. Sit down, straighten your legs, and place your right foot on the left side of your left thigh. Pull it in toward your body, and then twist your body as far to the right as you can without overdoing it. Reverse this by putting your left foot to the right side of your right thigh and twisting to the left.

Thigh stretches. Kneel on both knees with your feet below your butt. Now lean back as far as you can go, trying to touch the back of your head to the ground. This exercise stretches your thighs so that you can snap over the top of low bunkers by doing modified sit-ups and stretches your legs for kneeling in awkward positions. It also stretches your ankles so that you will be less likely to hurt them by leaning, laying, or running at strange angles.

Calf stretches. Find a car tire, tree, building, or other immobile object. Lean back and place the sole of your foot against the object, your heel on the ground, and lean forward. This will stretch your calves, and is a very important stretch to ensure maximum speed in running without seriously hurting yourself. Switch feet and repeat until both legs are completely stretched.

Upper thigh stretches. Standing on your left foot, supporting yourself by grabbing onto a tree if you must, grab your right foot with your right hand and pull your heel toward your butt. Keep your back straight to prevent injury, and then similarly stretch your left leg. The goal here is to stretch the muscles of your upper legs, which are powerful muscles that give you speed on the field and help you snap from position to position behind your bunkers…keep them in top shape!

With your body stretched, there is only one measure left to take: get your heart pumping to push adrenaline throughout your body. Who will run faster, a man off the street, or a guy who's spent the morning taking a few practice laps and preparing for a race? Obviously, the guy who prepared…but many paintball players still go into games without warming up, stretching out, or readying their bodies in any way. Professional football players, soccer stars, baseball players, hockey players—even many professional paintball players—all warm up before their games! Get your heart racing before the start horn, and you'll be in the game immediately instead of still ramping up when the paint hits the air.

Get that heart rate up! Jog one lap around the staging area, at a medium pace (no use tiring yourself out, but just walking is not as helpful). This gets your body ready for sprinting. Now drop down and do a half set of pushups (half as many as the maximum you can do…you don't want to tire out your arms before the game). Your blood is now rich with oxygen and adrenaline, and is pumping strongly. Your body is ready for immediate action. Look at the pansies across the field: they still have donut crumbs on their lips and restful heart rates. They aren't even a challenge to you.

PAINTBALL WORKOUT

What do you need to win? Speed, stamina, accuracy, intelligence, and reliable gear. You can buy a good marker, practice awesome moves at the field, and improve your shooting skills at the range. Speed and stamina come from determined improvement: working out, and dedication to healthy living.

Get your body in tournament, or big game, shape by jogging. Your goal should be to jog at least one mile a day, two if you can, three days a week with an off day in between. Individuals may be able to run farther more frequently, but set a minimum of one mile three days a week, as your initial goal. Start slowly by running as far as you can at a medium pace, and when you feel fatigued, any pain, or excessive shortness of breath, stop. Look at your distance: a few feet? A quarter mile? Make that the distance to beat every day, and then walk as briskly as you can until you feel comfortable running again. Finish the mile in this manner.

Pace a mile with the odometer in a car: drive the route you plan to jog, measuring from a fixed starting point (your driveway, perhaps the edge of a school or Post Office) and finding a fixed end point at your desired distance.

Warm up for your run by walking at a brisk pace for several hundred feet, and then after you cease running, walk briskly for another few hundred feet as a "cool down" to keep your muscles from slamming between the extremes of "sprint" and "stop." If you feel up to jogging again, do so, stopping to walk when you feel the need.

Once you can jog a mile without stopping, time your run. Each time you run, try to beat your fastest time…if even by only one second. Through dedication to meeting and breaking distance and time goals, you will be able to jog your full goal and notice a marked improvement in your overall health.

Jogging builds your speed on the field, and also helps get your heart, lungs, and muscles in shape for extended periods of hard use: tournaments, scenario games, and even open play in the woods.

Strength training is less important in paintball than in other sports, though good upper body strength helps prevent injuries, and can help you shoot more accurately at the end of the day. Ever pick up a marker that is simply too heavy for you to carry for any length of time? Build muscle mass through careful exercises and you will be able to hoist and haul heavier gear.

Ever get the limp arm feeling toward the end of a long day? Tone your muscles and keep them in shape, and you will be able to snapshoot crisply all day long and avoid the shakes and droops that destroy late-day accuracy.

Underarm curls. Use free weights that are light enough so you can do seven to ten repetitions of a given exercise, but heavy enough that they give you a good challenge. Pick up one weight in each hand, making sure that the weights are equal. Never pick up only one weight at a time: the imbalance is very hard on your spine and the rest of your body. Lift the weight toward your armpit, curling your hand under as you go. Do one repetition with the right hand, then one with the left, then repeat for a set of seven to ten. Rest, and then repeat with another set.

Pull-ups. The author's favorite exercise, this is also one of the simplest exercises to perform. Find a pull-up bar, or the bottom rung of a fire escape, an erect ladder, or other horizontal bar securely fixed to something solid. Face your palms towards your body and lift yourself off of the ground. This improves bicep strength. Face your palms out when you grab the bar and these pull-ups will improve your deltoid strength—the muscles that you use to climb over bunkers and scale walls. For each, lift your body until your chin is just over the bar, then slowly let yourself back down. Repeat.

Butterflies. Find a resistance machine, and under the supervision of a trainer or health monitor, use this machine to build pectoral (chest muscle) strength. The basic exercise of bringing your hands together horizontally, in front of you, with great resistance, will increase the strength of the muscles in your chest.

Sit-ups. Don't have a flat stomach? Don't worry about it: let the guys who have nothing better to do with their social lives live in the gym trying to fight the natural curves of their abdomen. You're here to get strong for paintball, and strength comes from having healthy muscle in good condition. Performance, not vanity, is what we seek. Lie down on your back, on a mat, with your legs out in front of you. Scrunch your knees up toward your chest, dragging your feet toward your butt. Now lift your feet and head off the mat. Put your arms across your chest, hands holding their opposite shoulders. The exercise: make your elbows touch your knees.

This is a modified sit-up often referred to as a "crunch," and offers great strength training and toning without many of the associated lower back problems reportedly caused by traditional sit-ups. There are resistance machines that mimic these exercises while putting your body in more ergonomic positions (sitting up, for example, and bending down), but they accomplish the same thing that you can accomplish on the floor at home or on a padded mat at a small gym. Do a maximum set of sit-ups, rest, and repeat, like with all exercises.

Pushups. A favorite punishment in boot camp, the threat of high school gym teachers—and one of the most convenient ways of building upper body strength—is the dreaded pushup. Lie face down on the ground, and plant your hands in front of your shoulders, palms to the dirt. Keeping your back straight, push yourself up until your arms are fully extended. Now lower yourself gently to the ground, and count "one!" Repeat until you cannot comfortably, and with good form (full arm extension, straight back), continue, then rest.

Circuit training is a good way to use machines at many gyms, and with good reason: by spreading sets of exercises between different targeted areas of the body, you give muscles a chance to relax and recover between sets while working other groups, and not wasting time. Circuit training involves doing one set of an exercise, such as a bench press exercise, then performing one set of another, such as a leg press, followed by a third, like an abdominal workout, and then returning to the first exercise to begin a second "circuit."

In the end, you do the same amount of the same exercises, often in less time, and you do not obliterate your strength in any one area all at once. Circuit training is great for building and toning muscle, as well as preventing workout-related injuries.

GAMES WE PLAY

CAPTURE THE FLAG

This classic format was used in the first paintball games ever played, and remains the most prevalent. There are many subtle variations wrapped around the concept of capturing your opponents' flag.

Two teams start at opposite ends of a playing field. This area, called a flag station or starting station, could be a developed base or simply a rope tied between trees. It is marked with the team's flag (a bandana, dishcloth, or actual flag). The purpose of the game is for the teams to cross the field while engaging their opponents, and then steal their opponents' flag. To win, they usually must take the flag back to their own flag station.

A majority of tournaments use the center flag version of this idea, where there is only one flag in the game, and it hangs in the center of the field. To win, one team captures the flag from the center of the field and runs it to their opponents' starting station.

Another variation that harkens back to the origins of the sport finds each player, or group, with a unique flag and separate starting station. Players are not allowed to move the flags at their starting station. The object of this game is for each group to capture as many flags as they can without getting shot. The player or group that captures the most flags wins.

TOURNAMENTS

A vast majority of tournaments are held on speedball fields, and feature competition for teams with ten, seven, five, four, three, or two players, while some tournaments also feature "Top Gun" divisions for one-on-one contests. Ten and seven player formats use a two flag system, in the traditional capture and return style. Five and fewer player formats typically use the center flag model.

In standard tournament paintball, with the exception of X-Ball, points are awarded to the team that pulls the flag first (twenty points), to the team that hangs the flag (fifty points), and then for each elimination and each "live" player at the end of the game so that the total points possible add up to 100.

X-Ball is a tournament format where teams compete for one point per game, awarded to the team that hangs the center flag on their opponents' starting station. Matches are divided up into two halves, with equal time limits counted down on a special electronic scoreboard. Teams switch sides of the field at halftime. Each match is comprised of numerous games.

A starting horn begins the action and the clock for each game. Players attempt especially aggressive, high-stakes moves in X-Ball because individual players are not worth points—teams only need one live player to hang the flag for the point after eliminating their opponents. When the flag hits the start station, the clock stops and teams have a minute and a half to gather fresh pods, fill their air, clean their goggles, and regroup to begin the next match.

X-Ball is unique to tournament paintball in that coaches are allowed to coach their teams during the game, and any spectators are welcome to yell at and coach players during the action. Players can rotate into the games during the ninety second break after each point, fielding fresh players with different specialties. Designated pit crews work beside the field, behind safety netting, to clean markers, fill pods, and refresh air tanks to keep the players competitive for the length of the game.

Get the first pull points if it's the last move you make!

SCENARIO GAMES

Players fantasize endlessly: they are soldiers behind the lines in a long past war, or Space Marines fighting to save the planet, or...Scenario games drive a large part of the paintball industry, and their players are particularly hardcore about paintball. These games are generally large affairs where players of all ages and types turn up to dress as and act the parts of special characters on specific missions.

The heart of the scenario game, from record setting affairs to five player outings on private land, is the storyline: players become more than "blue team" and "red team." They adopt certain identities, like soldiers, aliens, mafia hit men, FBI agents, etc. Teams have specific missions and goals that follow a storyline. At an International Amateur Open scenario game, the Army of the Blues fought government agents to secure financial prosperity for their music. Every year at the Bunker Xtreme in Oklahoma and Skirmish USA in Pennsylvania, thousands of players don

WWII fatigues and battle in the spirit of the D-Day invasion of Normandy.

For playing on a smaller-than-epic scale, let your imagination run wild the day before the action. Concoct an attention-grabbing storyline—it could be fantasy, military, folklore, or even inspired by video games or music. Take volunteers to play certain critical characters in your storyline, and divide up and issue armbands that identify each player's team allegiance.

Blue's Royal Platter, one of ten props used in EMR's bi-annual Castle Conquest games

The more elaborate the plot, to a point, the more the players can immerse themselves in their characters and the storyline. Props help, such as wooden dowel rods painted red to resemble dynamite, fake money bundled together, etc. Some players, such as the Woodland Warriors scenario team, have a lively fascination with fabricating functional tanks! There is virtually no end to the role playing, pageantry, complexity, and fun of playing in scenario games.

NIGHT PLAY

A flare thumps into the sky, breaking with a loud crack. Everything lights up in an eerie orange glow—there is a base full of opponents straight ahead! Paint flies from dozens of markers, but in the flare-shadowed night all you hear are the thwacks of balls hitting trees and goggles. The flare burns out and all is dark again, yet the shooting continues. Time to move: flank the base so you can shoot from behind when the next flare pops!

Night games are awesome, and some players say that night missions are the best part of scenario games. Some field owners are willing to host night games as special events if you offer to help organize the game and bring in additional players. With dark falling early in the autumn, you can manage several games in a night without staying up too late…or wait for a warm summer evening and find a local scenario game with action through the midnight hour!

Playing at night poses various challenges, from safety (you can't see holes as well in the dark) to keeping a unit together (ever try keeping twenty people together while moving through a dark forest?) and coordinating well-timed attacks. Regular camouflage patterns work very well for concealment at night, so players end up scattered everywhere ambushing anyone who comes near! The confusion is exciting, so long as you don't take the game too seriously, and you keep your mask on the entire time.

BIG GAMES

There is nothing like the thrill of a big game packed with players! Hundreds, sometimes thousands of players battling together is the draw for these massive-scale events. Some big games have scripted storylines like scenario games, while others simply pit one team against another in a contest for various positions around a huge playing field.

These events are not the sorts of things you can organize on a whim, but for something different and exciting, check the paintball media for announcements of coming big games in your area. Be sure to bring a camera!

Part of the thrill comes from using tanks, and dressing for the roles

STOCK

Stock class markers are pumps that have feed tubes mounted to their bodies instead of hoppers, and use 12gram disposable CO_2 cartridges instead of CO_2 bottles or compressed air tanks. As these three limitations slow the rate of fire and limit the capability of sustained fire (around thirty shots per 12gram is average, and most stock class markers only hold ten balls at a time), it drastically changes your style of play. There is no such thing as accuracy by volume with pump markers, and the ability to shoot cover fire is greatly inhibited.

Stock class players often wear special harnesses that hold ten round tubes of paint and extra 12gram CO_2 powerlets for fast reloading in the field. Their overall paint usage is drastically lower than when they play with semiautomatics: most stock players shoot fewer than three hundred paintballs per day.

Stock class games are played like any other paintball game: in the woods, on speedball courses, in scenario games, in stock class only tournaments…the options are virtually endless. Part of what makes this format so much fun is that the benefits of high rates of fire and accuracy by volume are stripped away. Suppressing lanes is difficult with a rate of fire around one ball per second. This allows players to move frequently, resulting in dynamic game play with ever-changing angles. The basic skills of moving, accurate shooting, timing, team work, and cunning strategy are the core of playing well in stock class games!

Some players appreciate how overshooting is virtually unheard of in stock class play—seldom does a player get hit more than once in a game.

TOTAL ELIMINATION

Popular for speedball and many open play games, this game is very straightforward: a team wins by eliminating all of their opponents. Two teams start at opposite ends of the field, or individual players/squads start staggered around the tapeline.

Last man standing competitions are fun to play after one team wins a regular game. When one team is completely eliminated, have the referee yell, "Last man standing in three, two, one, go go go!" This starts the every-man-for-himself game. The last player still in the game is the ultimate winner.

SEARCH AND DESTROY

The enemy has a cache of almost-completed experimental weapons. Your crack unit volunteered to lead an expedition into the heart of enemy territory to seek and destroy their facility. Grab your gear and move out!

This format is the classic "find something and blow it up" mission, but with a fun technological twist: when field conditions are favorable, each searching team should be armed with several smoke grenades. When the game begins, players search the field for a particular base or area that is designated as the target (with a flag or props), neutralizing opponents along the way. To destroy the target, they must set off a smoke grenade within the compound or next to a designated building. Each team can hunt for the opponents' base, or teams can have specific attack and defend roles.

FOX AND HOUND

It's you versus them, winner take all as you play the wily fox setting ambushes for the pack of hounds. Or perhaps you are a downed pilot, trapped behind the lines and vastly outnumbered with no choice but to shoot your way out!

This is a hunting style game where one player, or a small squad, is designated the "fox" or the "downed pilot" and given time to hide on the field. The rest of the players form one united team, the "hounds," to flush and eliminate their quarry.

Many players enjoy this format for the challenge of using tactical skills to clear buildings and secure areas of the field. Tactically minded foxes find inventive ways to ambush players, such as burying themselves in leaves, minimizing noise by barrel tagging players instead of shooting them, and hiding in implausible places. This is definitely for your inner Rambo: an opportunity to single-handedly challenge an entire force!

BEHIND THE LINES

Over the radio comes a faint cry for help from your Special Operations teammate: his squad is down, and now he's alone behind enemy lines with hostile players swarming the area. He cannot escape alone, so you volunteer to lead an elite unit deep into hostile country to extract one of your own. The game is afoot!

On a standard field, start with the defending team scattered however they desire across one end-third of the field, with your lone teammate hiding somewhere among them (let him go out first and hide). Your team should start close together at the opposite end of the field, as if playing a normal game. At the "go" signal, the field goes live.

The object of this game is for your team to rescue your player, without that player getting shot. You have a finite amount of time, such as fifteen minutes, in which to sweep the field, eliminate any opponents you find, and rescue your teammate. He needs to escape from hostile territory, link up with your team, and make his way toward your starting station…all without getting hit.

In an ideal game, you will meet up with him and provide cover for his escape, then send one player to run with him back to your start station to end the game. But like any rescue behind enemy lines, things never go quite as planned.

RESCUE

One of your teammates was captured by the opponents in the last game. Now he is being held at their base, and you must rescue him before time runs out. Strike fast, because you only have a few minutes to liberate your teammate…and strike smart, or they might get nervous and shoot him!

This game is great for an odd number of players, where the odd man out is a natural choice to play the prisoner. The capturing team takes the field first, with their unarmed prisoner in tow, and establishes a base wherever they like. The liberating team enters the field, cautiously searching for their teammate and fighting valiantly to liberate him.

The captors win if time expires and they still have the prisoner…provided the prisoner has not been shot. The liberators win if they get the prisoner to a designated "safe area." If the prisoner gets shot by either team at any time, both teams lose.

The fun twist on this game is that the prisoner can attempt an escape and at any time get shot by his captors. The prisoner faces a tough choice: attempt an escape and risk a game-ending elimination, or stay put and risk remaining a "live" captive when the time runs out, winning the game for his opponents. If the rescuing team runs out of time with no hope of a last-second victory, they might try to shoot the prisoner to avoid the other team getting the win! With so many variations, this game stays fresh time and again.

Actually rescuing a player and conveying him back to safety is a great change from capturing a flag...and it's really challenging to play the prisoner!

PROTECT THE PRESIDENT

A pack of mad gunmen bent on assassinating the President stalk through the forest around Camp David. Your job as a Secret Service agent is to stop them and protect your President at all costs.

Designate one team as the Secret Service and task them with protecting the President. The remainder of the players, either equal in size or much more numerous, attempt to assassinate the President. The Secret Service wins if the President remains "alive" for an allotted amount of time. The bad guys win if they shoot the President.

A paintball assassin's tool—an electro marker built into a briefcase with an electronic trigger in the handle!

More dynamic games involve transporting the President across the field while the opposing forces lie in ambush. The Secret Service team wins when they get the President safely to their objective, such as a flag station.

This format is great for parties, as the birthday person, bachelor, etc, can be assigned the dubious honor of being the President. With large enough groups, you can have a President on each team and divide the groups between offensive and defensive forces.

CASTLE DEFENSE

The attacking army outside your castle taunts you for a second time. They want to take your castle, depose your king, and sully your damsels! This cannot stand! Defend your kingdom!

Fields with actual castles are great, but rare. You can designate any developed base or complicated bunker as a castle and then play a game of attack and defend. The defending team should put players outside of the castle to prevent attackers from using paint-grenades and storming the bastion. Attacking teams should circle around the structure to take advantage of an uneven dispersal of defenders or any weakness in the fortification.

Defending teams win when they hold the castle for a set period of time. Attackers win when they change a flag in the castle to their team's color, by eliminating all the defenders, getting more of their players into the castle than there are remaining defenders, or by setting off a smoke grenade inside the structure. The more creative the rules, the more fun the game!

TAKE AND HOLD

Winter is coming, and your team needs food and shelter. There is a fort over yonder full of food and warm buildings, but it's occupied by hostile forces! Realizing that your men are in desperate need, you order an attack.

This variation of attack and defend offers the opportunity for ousted defenders to regain control of their territory. One team starts in and around a base or specifically defined area. The other team must capture this stronghold within a certain time limit. Whoever has a simple majority, or a complete domination (depending on your rules) of the area when time runs out, wins.

This format works especially well in scenario games or other events where long games with individual missions are normal. Player reinsertions add to the excitement, as defenses can be reinforced and offensive units can regroup to try repeated attacks. The swinging balance of power keeps the action intense to the end!

Tourney players can forgo the prologue and play this game on speedball fields, where one team occupies a complex structure like a snake or a cluster of standup bunkers while another team attacks from enterprising angles.

Go ahead—wear a costume, and be a Mexican bandit if you want! Ponchos promote bounces, after all...

RUN THE GAUNTLET

The field is in enemy control, and the only way out is down a narrow path between two fortified emplacements. Your opponents are strong, and their aim is true. Winners need courage, cunning, and teamwork to get players through a gauntlet of hostile fire.

Select a field that has two easily defended positions, such as bases or steep hills, set ten to thirty yards apart. The gauntlet team splits up and takes control of these two positions. The escape team enters the field, and has a limited amount of time to get their entire team through the space between the fortifications. Think of a field goal in football, with the forts as the goal posts and your players as footballs…only these goal posts shoot at you when you try to score!

The "escaping" team can flank the fortifications if they like…but only players who run between the fortifications and get through unscathed are counted for score. The escaping team risks running out of time and players if they get bogged down in the battle. This game rewards decisive moves, strategy, small group tactics and coordinated suppressive fire.

Run this game twice so that each team gets a turn at escaping and defending. Keep track of the number of players who get through for each team. The greater number wins.

RAIDERS

Everywhere on the speedball field, or behind all those woodsball bunkers, lies treasure: diamonds, gold, rare crystals…The opportunity for riches is magnificent, but the dangers from natives and other raiders are immense!

The referee declares certain objects, such as brightly painted cans, custom made props, or even rolls of paper towel, to be the "treasure" that teams clamor after. Different point values can be awarded to add another level of strategy to this already complex game of paintball fetch!

Two teams can play, or multiple squads, or each player for

themselves. One team (or a referee for every-man-for-himself games) is allowed five minutes on the field to hide the treasure: but they have to keep one player guarding it until he is eliminated, and he may not move unless he brings the treasure with him.

Holding onto the treasure for the duration of the game (five, ten, fifteen, or twenty minutes depending on the size of the group) secures points for the defending team, while the capturing team receives the points for having treasure in their control at the end of the game. In multiple-squad games, the teams challenge each other while scampering to secure as much treasure as possible!

Every man for himself versions of this game are interesting, as two or three players may make alliances on the fly…and break allegiances at their will! Players begin from various places around the field, and at "go" they raid, plunder, and eliminate each other as needed.

CIVIL WAR

Gettysburg, July 2nd, 1863. You place a single paintball in the muzzle of your marker and push it home with your squeegee, then stare at your opponent without a hopper in the way. There are thirty yards and a few trees between the line of Union players and Major General George Pickett's line of Confederates. The first marker goes off, and everyone opens fire! The battle is on, with rapid reloading and one-shot-hits!

Paintballs must be single loaded, by hand, just like muskets in the Civil War. You can either drop them into the chamber one by one to get something of the musket effect, or for maximum authenticity and fun, muzzle-load each ball and push them back to the chamber with your squeegee!

Maneuvering your forces is very important, as players cannot rely on high rates of fire or dumb luck to win! Movement is essential, and with such a limited amount of paint (and maximum amount of taunts!) in the air, bold moves are easier to make and more fun to try! Play around with the objectives, as you can make these games total elimination, capture the flag, survive the gauntlet, or any other permutation imaginable.

Consider this format for the end of the day when players don't have many paintballs left, or to warm up in the morning and get everyone thinking about movement, angles, and accuracy. Young players who initially hesitate to face experienced players in open play often embrace this game because it removes the intimidation factor of high cyclic rates.

Go all out with this idea by staging games where teams start forty yards apart across an open field, facing each other, just like the Revolutionary and Civil wars! On the command "go go go" players either shoot or run. This is not a format for everyday play, but give it a try as a novelty or to better envision what these historic battles might have been like.

POKER

Before you can hold 'em, fold 'em, or walk away, you've gotta run straight into the casino and grab a heapin' handful of cards. But those gamblers are a tough bunch, and won't just give away their best hands...you've gotta take 'em by force.

Each player draws a card from a standard deck, then carries the card onto the field. Large groups can split into small teams that start staggered around the field, in a standard two-team skirmish, or in a free-for-all knockout. When hit, players remove their cards and set them on the ground. The player who made the shot can claim that card...if he can get to it before anyone else!

Use an especially short time limit on these games so that they end with several players still "live." A player wins by having the strongest poker hand under stud rules: they can use a maximum of five cards, despite how many they actually have.

When you have too few players to make a go of the one-card-per-elimination rule, have a referee go around the field putting cards in obvious and highly visible places. At the start horn, each player scrambles to collect the best hand he can while engaging the other players.

Perhaps you'll invoke the rule that no player can carry more than five cards at a time, and make them choose which ones to take, which to leave, and force even more commotion and moving around on the field!

CHRISTMAS IN AUGUST

Named for the Christmas in August tournament held annually at Xtreme Paintball Park in Millstadt, Illinois, this format essentially throws paintballs out the window while retaining the other elements of our sport. Any speedball or woodsball tournament format may be used, from top gun to ten or fifteen player teams, with the appropriate scoring for eliminations, active players, first pull, and hang.

The difference between this game and others comes in the equipment used: standard goggles, of course, but unloaded markers…and various hand-to-hand objects strewn about the field. Teams begin each game without any paint, and at "go," scramble across the field to any of a large quantity of paint cases. Inside of these "Christmas presents," are various objects from tennis balls to foam darts, squirt guns to toy swords and water balloons…only one box per side of the field contains paintballs, and at that, it contains no more than one paintball per opposing player.

Elimination rules are similar to standard tournament rules, where a US Quarter-sized mark of water is required to eliminate a player. Players may also be eliminated by being touched with the plastic sword, hit with a foam ball, etc. Clever players capitalize on the "Jedi Knight" rule, where they block throwable objects, paintballs, etc, with the toy swords, if they can! Reffing the game presents a challenge unto itself …

This format has little to do with strategy, but when the paint is low and all you care about is fun, there are few better ways to get an afternoon of laughs with friends. Try this format as a fund-raiser when you have paintball-shy participants—they won't get shot much, if at all, but will have an amazing time chasing each other around a speedball field with dodge balls and toy swords!

BOMB SQUAD

Your SWAT team is down to fifteen minutes before the bomb goes off…and you still haven't found it. Somewhere in an area secured by terrorists and crooks is a tactical nuclear warhead that is about to wipe out several city blocks!

Buy a used briefcase at a second hand store, then spend some time with batteries, flashlight bulbs, and wires—all available for a few dollars total at your local hardware store. Rig a simple circuit in the suitcase so that the batteries power the light, and install a simple switch to turn the light on and off. The bad guys get to hide this "bomb" wherever they please, then defend it for the duration of the game against the Bomb Squad team. Have them turn the light on during the action, so that the good guys must actually manipulate something to "disarm" the bomb.

With enough players, you can designate one or two special players as "bomb technicians," and instigate the rule that only these players can disarm the bomb. If they get eliminated during the action, that's it—the bad guys win! Keep your technicians alive and get them to the bomb before it goes off!

Hardcore scenario players love this format, and some have designed "bomb" briefcases that involve complex wiring and multiple lights to indicate when it is "armed," "neutral," and when it "detonates," so that disarming it requires more than simply cutting a wire or flipping a switch. Often games with these complex electronic props involve a side mission to capture disarming instructions from a second location on the field. This adds more action and suspense...and the instructions can really help your team's bomb technician!

DAY OF THE DEAD

Two zombies stumbled from the local graveyard onto the field, and now they're eating all the newbies! It's up to the still-living to stop the massacre!

Start this game with the entire group opposing two individual players. Every player wears an armband, except the two zombies. At game on, the zombies charge onto the field and engage the group. Any "living" player shot by a zombie instantly becomes a zombie, and indicates his change by pulling his armband off. Now they join the zombies in attacking the living!

All zombies are eliminated with one shot from a "living" player. Have a short time period for this game, and determine a winner by counting the players on each side when time runs out. Or, have a longer time period and wait for one side to completely eliminate the other!

Costumes help scenario players get in the mood—such as The Frog, French Commander at the Skirmish Invasion of Normandy...

MARKSMANSHIP

Some days it's you against the world; others, it's just you alone in it. For the times when you can only find a buddy or two, practice your marksmanship so you can hit anything that moves. Go to the range at your paintball field, or find a safe range to use, and set up a variety of targets from soda cans to paper cups to baseballs and anything else you don't mind painting up.

Set the targets at various ranges, and then play the classic basketball game of "P-I-G" or "H-O-R-S-E." Pick out a target, the more challenging the better, and call your shot: "soda can, fifteen yards out, right down the open mouth." You each shoot the target, and anyone who misses the called shot gets a sequential letter ("P" or "H," or "I" or "O" if it is their second miss, etc). If no one makes the shot, no one gets a penalty letter. The first player to spell "PIG" or "HORSE" loses…the last player in the running wins.

Look to the world of competitive shooting for other ideas, such as engaging a series of targets at various ranges as fast as you can. Find a field that is not in use at the time, and with a referee's blessing, set targets around the bunkers. Use a stopwatch to time how long it takes each shooter to hit each target. Complicate the drill by adding required moves, bunker runs, mandatory reloads, and other challenges!

GLOSSARY

Airsmith, n. One who is certified to work on compressed gas lines and components, such as the internal parts of a marker, or an air reservoir.

Amateur, adj. A player who has competed for more than four years, and does not claim the rank of "professional."

Armband, n. Fabric or plastic tied around your arm to denote, by color, the team you play for.

Automatic, adj. A type of marker, or shooting mode, wherein one trigger pull results in the discharge of two or more paintballs. Traditionally, "fully automatic" means that the marker will continue to shoot until the trigger is released.

Back Player, n. A competitor who plays near the rear of the team's formation, often in a support role.

Ball Detent, n. The device in the chamber of a paintball marker that detains a paintball in the chamber until shot.

Barrel, n. The portion of your marker through which a paintball is accelerated

Barrel Break, n. The condition when a paintball disintegrates in your barrel

Battle Swab, n. A fuzzy barrel cleaning device designed to soak up and brush away paint after barrel breaks.

Big Game, n. A game format that involves a large number of players, generally several hundred or more, and is not otherwise classified as a scenario game.

Bingo Ball, v. When the paint in your feed neck bounces up and down.

Bonus Ball, v. To shoot a player after he has been eliminated.

Bore, n. The inside of your barrel. Most paintball bores are smooth; some have straight rifling, while others have spiral rifling.

Bottomline, n. The marker setup where a tank screws into an ASA under the grip frame and is thus held parallel to and inline with the marker.

Bounce, n. When a paintball impacts a player, then ricochets off of them without breaking.

Bounce, v. On electronic markers, this is shooting with your hand in such a position that the recoil of the marker knocks the trigger against your finger, discharging the marker almost automatically.

BPS, abr. This is the abbreviation for "Balls Per Second," used to discuss how many paintballs a marker can shoot in one second.

Break, n. 1. A mark left on a player from a paintball impacting their body and leaving a mark of paint. Breaks must be at least the size of an American quarter dollar coin to eliminate a player. 2. The beginning of a game, when players "break" from the starting station to charge the field.

Bunker, n. The obstacle behind which you are hiding. They are often inflatable in speedball, or made of logs in woodsball.

Bunker, v. To charge a player's bunker and shoot him at pointblank range.

Burst Disk, n. A small piece of copper that covers a special hole in a tank regulator. It ruptures when the tank pressure becomes unsafe, preventing an explosion by venting the contents of the tank.

Can, n. A cylindrical bunker that resembles a can.

Chop, v. To pinch a paintball between the bolt and the feed port, breaking it in the chamber.

Chronograph, n. A device used to measure the velocity of paintballs.

Chronograph, v. To shoot your marker over a chronograph for the purpose of measuring the velocity of the paintballs.

Clown Paint, n. A mixture of different colors of paintballs in the same hopper.

CO2, n. Carbon Dioxide, which is the most poplar propellant gas used in paintball. It is measured in ounces while it is still in a liquid state.

Compressed Air, n. Compressed atmospheric air is a very popular propellant gas, and is measured in pounds per square inch of pressure.

Concealment, n. That which will hide your position, but not stop a paintball, such as light brush.

Cover, n. That which will stop a paintball, such as a solid bunker.

Cover, v. To shoot paintballs at an opponent so that a teammate, or you, may move with less danger.

Cover Fire, n. A volume of paint shot towards an opponent so that the shooter or a teammate may advance without being engaged.

Dead Box, n. Where players must go for the remainder of the game after being eliminated in a tournament.

Eliminate, v. To shoot a player and have a paintball break on their gear or body, resulting in their elimination from the game.

Expansion Chamber, n. A device that gives liquid CO_2 additional volume in which to expand into gaseous form, preventing the introduction of liquid CO_2 into a marker.

Eyes, n. Actually a misnomer, the "eyes" in your marker are lasers in your chamber. When the laser beam shoots across the chamber and impacts a sensor, the sensor tells your marker not to shoot, as there is no ball in the chamber (it might be only halfway in, and releasing the bolt would cause a chop).

Feed Neck, n. The part of the marker that conveys paintballs from the hopper to the chamber and holds the hopper onto the marker.

First Bunker Position, n. The first bunker that a player occupies at the beginning of a game.

Flag, n. A cloth or plastic flag that teams try to capture.

Flag Station, n. Where the flag hangs at the start of the game. In two-flag games, the opponent's flag must be brought to your own flag station.

Flank, n. The rear, side area of a group or position.

Flank, v. To move to and attack from the rear, side, position of your opponents' position.

FPS, abr. Feet Per Second, the measurement of the speed at which paintballs travel.

Front Player, n. A competitor who plays forward of the team's position, establishing a skirmish line.

Gogg, v. Slang for shooting a player in the goggles.

Goggles, n. The eye, ear, nose, throat, and face protection systems used in paintball.

Harness, n. The device players use to carry spare pods into games; also called packs.

Home Plate, n. A name for a pentagonal bunker that thus resembles home plate in baseball.

Hopper, n. The part of a marker that holds paintballs.

Hopper Cover, n. 1. A piece of cloth or plastic of a specific color that ties over the top of your hopper to identify your team. 2. Neoprene or other material surrounding your hopper to change its color, protect it from impact, or promote bounces.

Hot, adj. The term for a marker that shoots faster than the posted speed limit.

Hydro Test, n. A test performed on compressed air and CO_2 tanks to ensure that they are safe for operation.

Instinct Shoot, v. To shoot completely by feel, without the use of sights or other aids.

Key Bunker, n. A bunker that has good views on several important forward bunkers or flag stations.

Kill Count, n. A count of how many players have been eliminated. The more appropriate term is "elimination count."

Kneepad, n. Special protective gear worn on the knees that helps players dive, kneel, and crawl with a reduced risk of injury. Many kneepads in paintball also incorporate shin guards.

Lane, n. An open corridor between bunkers that connects one side or portion of a field to another.

Lane(ing), v. Shooting a steady stream of paintballs down a lane to suppress movement or hit advancing players.

Leading Edge, n. The edge of a bunker nearest to an opponent.

Leapfrog, v. To advance in such a manner that the rearmost aggressor advances to the forward-most position.

Marker, n. The device we use to shoot paintballs.

Mid Player, n. A competitor who plays in the middle of the team's formation, often in support of front players while also performing offensive roles.

Mine, n. A paintgrenade or other device rigged to go off when tripped instead of being thrown.

Neck Guard, n. Safety equipment in the form of a strap that winds loosely around a player's neck to protect the player's neck from paintballs.

Newbie, n. A player who has seldom or never played before.

Nitrous, n. Short for "nitrous oxide," a gas used in dental operations—absolutely never used in paintball. It is commonly confused as an incorrect slang term for "nitrogen," which is rarely used in paintball, in favor of regular compressed air.

Novice, adj. A player who has competed for between two and four years.

Open Play, n. A pickup game, where players meet randomly at the field. This is the form of play most often encountered by players who show up at local fields without a reservation.

O-Ring, n. A ring of plastic that is used to seal connections where compressed air is conveyed.

Out, adj. When a player is eliminated.

Overshoot, v. Shooting a player more times than necessary to eliminate him, normally defined by having more than four breaks on the player per barrel that shot at him.

Pack, n. See "Harness."

Paint Check, v. When a referee inspects a player to see if the player has been hit.

Paintball, n. A spherical gelatin capsule containing a non-staining, non-toxic marking compound.

Paintgrenade, n. A throwable device containing a liquid fill that sprays its contents upon impact.

Penalty, n. Punitive damages assessed against a player or team for breaking a rule. Penalties can include point subtractions, removal of active players from a game in progress, and ejection from events.

Playing On, v. When a player continues playing after being eliminated.

Pod, n. Cylindrical containers that hold extra paintballs for fast reloading during games.

Pod Up, v. To fill a pod with paintballs.

Pointblank, adj. A range of five feet or less.

Post(ing), v. Keeping your marker trained on a bunker without ducking back into your own bunker.

Powerfeed, n. An older-style offset hopper feed, where the hopper is suspended on one side of the marker (frequently the left) while the paint is fed across the top of the marker, and then diagonally into the chamber from the other side.

Powering In, v. To shoot one's own cover fire while advancing.

PSI, abr. The abbreviation for "Pounds per Square Inch," referring to the pressure of compressed gasses.

Pump, adj. A type of marker where a forearm must be cycled fore and aft to cock the marker and load a paintball into the chamber for each shot.

Rate Of Fire, n. The number of balls a marker can shoot in a given time period, usually one minute. It is sometimes abbreviated as "ROF."

Recball, n. Short for "recreational paintball," these are the informal games played among friends or during open play.

Referee, n. The game official who monitors safety, enforces rules, performs paint checks, and begins and ends games.

Regulator, n. A device that alters the pressure of gas from a higher pressure to a lower pressure. Also known by the slang term "reg."

Reinsert, v. When scenario players reenter a game, normally after sitting out for a short length of time.

Reinsertion Point, n. The place where reinserting players may rejoin the game.

Rookie, n. A player in their first year of competition.

Rumble, v. To shoot a bunker, especially an inflatable bunker, repeatedly, producing a distinct rumbling sound.

Run Through, v. The maneuver executed when a player breaches the skirmish line and charges through the opponents' side of the field, shooting any opponent he sees.

Scenario Game, n. A game format where players must complete tasks and achieve objectives to win. They normally involve the casting of players in specific roles.

Semiautomatic, adj. The mode of shooting wherein one trigger pull results in exactly one paintball being shot.

Simultaneous Elimination, n. See "Trade."

Skirmish, n. 1. The antiquated term for paintball. 2. A popular term used outside of America as a term for woodsball. 3. One of the oldest paintball fields in the world, located in Pennsylvania.

Skirmish Line, n. A line drawn across the field midway between the forward-most players on each team.

Snake, n. A type of bunker that is significantly longer than it is tall. They are normally made from joining several horizontal bunkers.

Snapshoot, v. To quickly lean out of your bunker, shoot, and duck back in.

Speedball, n. A paintball format played on a small field with bunkers, sparse or no brush, few trees, and short time limits.

Spherical Gelatin Capsule Linear Accelerator, n. The pretentious term for a paintball marker.

Spin, v. When a player whirls around to shoot you, such as when a player you ask to surrender turns quickly to engage you. Spinning is cheating when you bunker a player, fairly eliminate him, and he whirls around to shoot you anyway.

Sponsorship, n. When a company provides a player or team with free or discounted goods or services in exchange for services and promotions.

Squeegee, n. A plastic device featuring a rubber disk that is used to clean paint from barrels after barrel breaks.

Start Station, n. Where teams cluster to begin games, and where the flag is hung in center-flag format games.

Stock Marker, n. A pump action marker that uses 12gram CO_2 powerlets and features a tube mounted to the body that holds less than 15 paintballs.

Strong Hand, n. The hand you write with.

Sweet Spot, v. To shoot a specific part of a bunker, lane, or other feature of a field, to hit a player. This usually involves shooting at targets obscured by distance or intervening bunkers, and letting them run into your stream of paint.

Tank, n. 1. A compressed air or CO_2 bottle. 2. A motorized vehicle used in paintball for the transport of players, or upon which is mounted markers or cannons.

Tapeline, n. The edges of a field, marked by boundary tape or rope.

Tournament, n. A structured competition wherein multiple players or teams compete. Most often, tournaments use the speedball format.

Trade, v. When two players eliminate each other at the exact same moment.

Tube, n. See "Pod."

Tunnel Vision, n. Focusing all of your attention on one player to the exclusion of what is going on everywhere else.

Valve, n. A device that controls the flow of pressurized gas. They are found inside markers, as well as in all tanks.

Velocity, n. The speed at which an object, such as a paintball, travels.

Weak Hand, n. The hand you do not write with.

Woodsball, n. Paintball played on forested fields, generally with long time limits.

About the Author

Dave Norman began playing in 1996 at Wacky Warriors in Millstadt, Illinois. In his first game he charged three players with a rental Tippmann SL68 pump and got lit up in grand style. Standing there dripping paint and stinging, he laughed like a madman and fell headlong in love with paintball.

Five years later he started writing for Action Pursuit Games magazine, discovered stock play at Xtreme Paintball Park, abandoned his other professional aspirations, and became a "paintball journalist."

Dave's articles have appeared in Action Pursuit Games, Facefull, Paintball Sports, Jungle, Paintball 2 Xtremes, Paintball News, Paintball Magazine, Warpig.com, and newspapers, literary magazines, and travel magazines around the country. A 2004 graduate of Westminster College, 2006 graduate of Dartmouth College's Masters of Arts in Liberal Studies program, and unapologetic international freeloader, he's hitchhiked to federal disaster areas and slept on couches around the world. Got a good story, and a soft place to sleep? Give him a call...